Moving Out of the Box

MOVING OUT OF THE BOX

Tools for Team Decision Making

Jana M. Kemp

Stanford Business Books
an Imprint of Stanford University Press
Stanford, California
2009

Stanford University Press
Stanford, California

First published in paperback in 2009.

Moving Out of the Box: Tools for Team Decision Making, by Jana M.
Kemp, was originally published in hard cover by Praeger Publishers,
http://www.greenwood.com/praeger, an imprint of Greenwood
Publishing Group, Inc., Westport, CT. Copyright © 2007 by Jana
M. Kemp. This paperback edition by arrangement with Greenwood
Publishing Group, Inc. All rights reserved.

Library of Congress Cataloging-in-Publication Data
Kemp, Jana M.
    Moving out of the box : tools for team decision making / Jana M.
Kemp.
        p. cm.
    Originally published: Westport, Conn. : Praeger, 2008.
    Includes index.
    ISBN 978-0-8047-6246-5 (pbk. : alk. paper)
    1. Teams in the workplace.   2. Group decision making
I. Title.   II. Title: Tools for team decision making.
HD66.K46   2009
658.4′036—dc22   2009005177

Special discounts for bulk quantities of Stanford Business Books
are available to corporations, professional associations, and other
organizations. For details and discount information, contact the special
sales department of Stanford University Press. Tel: (650) 736-1783,
Fax: (650) 736-1784

Contents

Preface

This book is about how to have and expand a conversation that leads to actionable decisions. Based on the ChoiceMarks language and decision-making process—"ChoiceMarks" provide new tools for expanding collaborative discussions and reaching consensus. This book makes problem solving and decision making less painful and more action oriented. As you'll see, consensus is not about having a war of words. And consensus and collaboration also sometimes require command-and-control decision making. Today's leaders must therefore be masters of command and control as well as consensus and collaboration in order to achieve ongoing success and stability of growth for a company, an organization, and even a country and the world.

In 2002, during a tedious volunteer board meeting in which the board struggled to make a decision, I held my frustrated tongue. As the conversation circled again and again, and a lack of decision making kept the group from moving forward, I noticed that many questions were left unanswered and that needed questions weren't being asked. Some voiced the frustrations they felt, while others held them inside. I could see that the meeting leader and the participants were struggling to make a decision and yet couldn't figure out how.

While in that meeting, I began reflecting on how decision making could benefit from a structure and grammar of sorts that is similar to our system of question marks and exclamation points. I realized that we already have question marks to seek out information, periods to say we've finished a thought, exclamation marks to add emphasis to a comment, commas to separate ideas, and quotation marks to show that someone is speaking or being quoted. So, I wondered, where are the marks that tell us someone needs more information before a decision can be made and that tell us what kind of decision someone is leaning toward making? ChoiceMarks—based on what I'd learned over two decades about decision making, coming to consensus, and getting groups unstuck and making decisions—were born.

When meetings bog down, teams fall apart, and individuals decline to budge on their positions, it is time to implement the ChoiceMarks for decision making. While writing this book, I discovered an eraser set of pink, blue, green, and purple question marks and exclamation points. This discovery supported my theory that we need some sort of grammatical marks to add to our decision-making toolboxes so that every member of a group can recognize where others are and can work together to get a decision made. More recently, I also found 3M's Post-it® page marker and pad sets. Blue, green, and orange, they sport question marks, exclamation marks, and quotation marks. This paper-based toolset prompted me to smile and think, "More tools for taking action and making decisions. This is good—people must be looking for ever-better tools!"

Sneak Peek at the Chapters Ahead

1. Introduction: How to Make Decision Making Easier

Chapter 1 contains examples of our difficulty in making decisions in today's fast-paced, information-overloaded environments—environments in which people seem to have forgotten their people skills and their ability to interact effectively.

2. Equal Decision-Making Processes: Command-and-Control and Collaborative Consensus

An overview of the decision-making processes that have been at war for more than 50 years, this chapter posits that today's leaders and team members need to master both approaches to decision making. You'll learn why both approaches are equally important and effective (and in Chapter 9 discover more details). Chapter 2 includes examples of groups that are stuck, followed by cause identification. It also includes a discussion of the kinds of individual and group personalities that can cause a group to get stuck and a quiz that allows you to identify your decision-making personalities.

3. ChoiceMarks Defined: Anti-Survival, Boxed-in, Neutral, Engaged Enthusiasm, Extreme Excitement

In Chapter 3, I define and illustrate each ChoiceMark. The chapter begins a discussion of moving individuals and groups from one ChoiceMark to the next, a discussion that the following chapters expand upon.

4. Managing Extreme Excitement

"Extreme excitement" is often the place that teams and group leaders think that they must get to in order to have agreement. But this is a rare group occurrence. In Chapter 4 you will learn to recognize and manage individuals and groups who reach this level of consensus.

5. Working with Engaged Enthusiasm

"Engaged enthusiasm" is a more common and occasionally more useful team reality. Part of the team will engage enough to move the decision forward and then follow through. In Chapter 5 you will learn to manage individuals and groups who are engaged and ready to act.

6. Moving Ahead with Neutral

Sometimes "neutral" is the best you can hope for when it comes to team decision making. In Chapter 6 you will learn to recognize when neutral is enough and how to inspire action even when people are in neutral.

7. Moving Out of Being Boxed-in

For decades we've heard about boxed-in thinking and the groupthink that prevents creative problem solving. In Chapter 7 you will learn to recognize boxed-in thinking and to ask the right questions to determine whether individuals and groups can move forward with a decision. Whether it is a go or no-go decision, clear decisions are needed so that each team member knows what responsibility rests on his shoulders and on her desk for action and work performance.

8. Listening to Anti-Survival for Good Decision Making

Sometimes the nay-saying, kill-the-idea, or "anti-survival" thinker is on track. In Chapter 8 you will learn to recognize when a group should be listening to the anti-survival comments. Also, learn the tools and language to move an anti-survival thinker to neutral, or even engaged enthusiasm.

9. Consensus-Driven Decision Making Versus Command-and-Control Decisions

Leaders of this millennium need to be equally strong consensus and collaboration builders as they are command issuers and control keepers. Command-and-control decisions can be quite acceptable when coming to consensus doesn't work. In Chapter 9 you will learn how to use command-and-control decision-making techniques without alienating others.

10. Which ChoiceMark Is Your Worldview?

Chapter 10 builds on the surveys in earlier chapters about how people have preferred mindsets but can shift mindsets to be as effective as possible in making decisions without losing their identities.

11. Make a Decision and Move!

The key to decision making is to make one. Then, keep moving and implementing all the while continuing to gather information, hold discussions and debriefing sessions, and to make new decisions as appropriate. You will learn these skills in Chapter 11.

Moving Out of the Box with ChoiceMarks

Born out of that volunteer meeting I attended, ChoiceMarks bring decision language to visual life and to the conversation table in ways that empower groups to make clear and best-possible decisions more effectively. Many teams get stuck because there is a lack of language for processing the ideas and emotions that have them stuck. ChoiceMarks are tools for conversation that allow individuals, dyads, and teams to explore whether action can be taken, a new direction is needed, or whether a stop-action is actually the best choice. As you'll see, ChoiceMarks lead to clear action. Refined over the years into the tools that you are about to discover—and tested with many groups and consulting clients—you can use ChoiceMarks to improve your team's daily decision making. I invite you to engage your enthusiasm and stretch outside of your usual thinking "box" enough to become excited about the tools you are about to discover. Then, apply them to your everyday decision making and watch the magic begin to work.

Acknowledgments

Writing a book depends on a team of contributors and editors. I am grateful for the stories and background contributed by Trish Terranova, Deni Hoehne, Jo Beecham, Judge Stephen Trott, countless workshop participants, engineers who wanted the ChoiceMarks to have different names, General Jim Brooks, and Cindy Peterson. I am grateful for Jeff Olson's work on a project he picked up with and moved to completion. Thanks especially to Jacquie Flynn, my editor at AMACOM for *NO! How One Simple Word Can Transform Your Life,* for suggesting that the ChoiceMark material could stand on its own as a book.

At the end of each day, coming to consensus on a decision or issuing a command-and-control decision rests upon getting out of the boxes we lock ourselves into. We need to gather enough ChoiceMark information to make decisions and reach our goals. Here's to your improved decision making and results.

Jana Kemp
Boise, Idaho
2007

CHAPTER **1**

Introduction: How to Make Decision Making Easier

In a world in which information constantly changes, conflicts, and generally inundates us, we are asked to make decisions with too much information and yet not enough of the right information. Every workplace is subject to this influx and overload of information. Even on roadways, we now face information overload. Cities across the country are seeing digital billboards installed with screens that change every eight seconds while there are cell phones, directional road signs, music playing, changing weather conditions, on-board car communication systems, GPS screens, and kids in the car. All of this creates high distraction for our drive-time experiences, when the focus is meant to be on the road and fellow drivers, pedestrians, and children moving to and from school. Today, most workers find themselves so overwhelmed before, during, and after work that being asked to make more decisions seems too daunting and even creates paralyzing stress. People are also so overwhelmed with information and data sorting demands that they move into self-prescribed boxes of thinking.

These thinking boxes are recognized by phrases such as "I can't," which means "I'm so overwhelmed I won't even listen to or look at more data to make another decision." Another phrase often heard when stress is running high is, "It won't work," which either means "We've tried it before and it didn't work so don't try it again," or it means, "We have no reason to change what we are doing now." A third phrase that communicates a person's thinking box is, "I can only do so much," which means the person has too many to-do list items and is not ready to take on any more assignments. A fourth phrase sometimes heard at work is, "No worries, the right things will get done," which means the person with the to-do list is trying not to let stress enter the equation and is communicating that maybe everything will not get done but the critical "right" things will get done (hopefully). And the fifth phrase, "Somehow it will all get done"—whether or not it actually does get done is another matter—is spoken by someone who believes that and may be pressing for everything to get done, perhaps including the wrong things.

These processing boxes for thought are really coping mechanisms of a kind. Why? When we are so overloaded that nothing ends up making sense, we structure our own rules for accepting information, making decisions, and ultimately for interact-ing with others. As you can see from the meanings of each phrase, personal rules are being applied as each person moves through the day.

A Constructive Decision Process: Essential to Success

The consideration and study of why and how people make decisions even makes the news from time to time. For example, the March 19, 2007, edition of *The Wall Street Journal* ran this headline: "How Understanding the 'Why' of Decisions Mat-ters." And it does matter because without details and supporting data, poor and even wrong decisions can be made. *Moving Out of the Box* is about getting as much infor-mation as is needed and relevant to making best-possible decisions that result in action. It acknowledges and explores three decision-making styles and five primary consensus stages of thinking about information in order to make consensus-driven decisions. This book offers ideas for listening more effectively to people with differ-ent points of view so that consensus on a best-possible decision can occur. This book also speaks to the need for a balanced use of consensus decision making and command-and-control decision making. There is a time and a place for each in daily decision making. And staying in the box of consensus-only or command-and-control-only decision making doesn't generate consistently best-possible decision making.

Books on negotiation, consensus, problem solving, and win-win solution finding abound. *Moving Out of the Box* is different because its premise is that more "com-manding collaborators in chief" are needed in our workplaces and in our govern-ments. This premise is supported by the discussions of command-and-control decision making in balance with consensus-driven decision making that uses the ChoiceMarks decision tool presented in the chapters ahead. To be a "commanding collaborator in chief" means that a person holds a decision-making position of power and authority; has mastered the skill sets of both command-and-control decision making as well as consensus-oriented decision making; has mastered the ability to discern when to use what decision-making approach; and has mastered guiding peo-ple into the successful implementation of decisions made.

How Did We Get Here?

Command-and-control decision making comes forward through the millennia as a tested decision-making approach. If something needs to be done, and if no one is act-ing to get things done, someone will command that the get-it-done action occurs. Command-and-control hierarchies prevailed well into the last century and were espe-cially observed and commented upon during the 1950s "yes-man" and "up-the-organization" style workplaces and cultures of decision making. During the 1960s and 1970s, classifying, coding, and problem-solving models as well as communication skills training came into the workplace as a part of daily employee experience. Then the team-oriented push of the 1980s quality circles affected how work was to be done in companies of all sizes. During the last two decades of the twentieth century, team-based everything and cross-training was the norm. Hiring, firing, performance reviews, project work, and decision making of all kinds were all pushed into team environments with varying degrees of implementation success. Even students in school began receiving team projects to complete for their final grades.

During the team-based, cross-training pushes of the 1980s, I recall having a trade association debate with colleagues in the employee training profession. "Of course every worker needs to be cross-trained, otherwise team building hasn't really occurred," said one woman. My response was, "If I'm going in for brain surgery, I really don't want the heart surgeon working on my brain. And if I need my car's engine block to be replaced, I'd prefer not to have the tire specialists dropping in the new engine. In other words, I don't think every employee needs to be cross-trained to perform every job in an organization." The debate carried on for 20 or 30 minutes with most of the group standing by the "cross-train for greatest team effectiveness" position. I held my ground and continue to hold the position that there are jobs which make sense for cross-training to occur so that a team can function effectively. And, there are jobs that should remain specialty jobs. Of course, there are skill sets that belong to a multitude of jobs, for instance, communication skills, problem-solving skills, and decision-making skills are among those for which we need general training. That's why the focus of *Moving Out of the Box* is on decision-making skills for both individuals and teams.

Then, before the last century ended, the 1990s saw "flattened organizations," "open book management," "downsizing," "rightsizing," and what felt like organizational chaos because employer loyalty to employees vanished. In the midst of all of these changes in the size and structure of organizations, technological demands on individual workers grew and team-driven work continued. Cell phones became and remain permanent body attachments. In fact, over the last decade, our technologies have contributed to a loss of people and interaction skills, making teamwork more difficult.

For instance, at a department store's customer service return counter one evening, a woman in front of me talked on her cell phone the entire time she was trying to return half a dozen items. She barely spoke to the customer service representative that she was standing right in front of. When I reached the counter I said, "On behalf of all people who do this to you—I apologize for their rudeness." I just couldn't believe what I had witnessed. The store's customer service employee smiled and said "Thank you. You'd be surprised just how many times that happens to us." Which prompted me to think of places such as service counters, banks, restaurants, and post offices that now have signs posted saying "no cell phones." These postings are a very good idea, because one rude person can cause delays and problems for many others.

Worse, over the last decade, the sense that cell phone calls and incoming emails are all urgent has contributed to a loss of recognizing emergencies. For a multitude of reasons, people have succumbed to the sense that technology-driven requests take priority over human interactions. A variety of workplace publications have run articles on the phenomena of "in-office emailing rather than walking to talk to each other." The diminished time spent on in-person interactions is contributing to diminished conversation, discussion, problem solving, and decision making. Furthermore, diminished human interaction skills contribute to family frustrations and community chaos; volunteerism declines along with workplace productivity losses and increased safety and health risks.

In any case, in this millennia, a balance of decision-making styles is needed because project teams are the rule rather than the exception in today's organizations. And team-driven work seems to be in greater balance with the renewed use of organizational hierarchy that makes more clear who is ultimately responsible for making decisions. At the same time, nearly constant job changes and ongoing reorganizations contribute to levels of personal disease and chaos that create decision and work-completion paralysis at times. Along with these individual challenges come the pressures of performance goals, conflicting agendas, and political jockeying, causing few teams to make superior decisions consistently. Instead, team members communicate poorly or not at all, avoid provocative discussion, occasionally stab each other in the back, or in many other ways forget that their job is to make decisions that help to lead the company forward.

In the last three decades, team driven consensus-oriented decision making has gone through rises and falls in popularity. Given the need for continued team decision making, the way to make good decisions is to have an expansive group conversation that leads to sound decisions and swift decision implementation. Sounds simple, but in most organizations, making a decision and seeing it through can become an exercise in frustration for managers and employees alike. At one end of the spectrum are purely command-and-control decisions, proclaimed from on high and implemented through the ranks. Without input or buy-in from those affected by the decision, this approach can lead to resentment and backlash. At the other end of the spectrum are purely collaborative, consensus decisions that often lead to inoffensive, weak choices and subpar results.

Moving Out of the Box builds on the belief that 2010 and beyond will see a balance of consensus-oriented and command-and-control decision making along with a growing number of commanding collaborators in chief. The decision-making processes used over the span of human existence have always had an endpoint in mind, the endpoint of "action will result from what we decide right now." Whatever process is used to get to a decision, the end result must be to keep doing things as they are done now or to begin doing things differently. Effective decisions result in action. Whether it is "keep the status quo" or "make changes and move ahead" it is still an action decision. Whether decisions are arrived at by consensus-oriented discussion, by voting or by a command to get something done, action and implementation are expected to follow the decision. There's a time and place for collaboration skills that reach consensus, and a time for command and control. And there is a time to integrate both decision approaches. Individual team members and teams need the know-how to make effective decisions that have a positive impact on their organization's results.

Challenged to Get and Stick to a Decision

How many times have you seen people make a decision? I mean really make a decision, commit to it, spend money on it, and then get things done. Or, do you see people decide, commit resources, and then begin the debate again as to whether it was the right decision? This redoing of a decision when none of the information has changed is a waste of time, energy, and resources. Once a decision has been made, stick with it. Keep moving forward. If new information comes forward that changes how work needs to be done, then make a new decision with the new information. Rehashing decisions that have already been made is a form of waffling or indecision that leads to frustration and productivity loss.

What about decisions that get made and the affected parties aren't told? How often is this happening in your organization or workplaces that you know about? Whether the reason for not telling is forgetfulness, willful noncommunication, or intentional undermining, failure to communicate decisions causes workplace breakdowns that can result in lost productivity, frustrations, and, worst case, death. The responsibility for communicating decisions ultimately rests with team leaders, meeting leaders, and supervisors. Producing team meeting minutes that include a decision summary and an assignment list that includes what is going to be done by whom and by what deadline is critical to team success. Distributing the minutes ensures that each team member knows what needs to be done and what their part in accomplishing implementation really is. When people know what needs to be done, the work is more likely to be completed.

Another decision challenge is not reaching a decision at all. Whether it is unwillingness to make a decision, lack of authority to make a decision, or failure to have the final decision maker's presence in the discussion, failure to make a decision to move forward leaves the team to keep doing what it is currently doing. One public-sector client of my company said, "We have a decision culture that most often results in no decisions being made in meetings. Either the right people are missing so a decision can't be made, or there is a general unwillingness among meeting attendees to make a decision." What is needed in this case is to get the right people to the meeting or cancel the meeting.

The following strategies will help you get the right people to the meeting with the readiness to make a decision.

Basic Meeting Guidelines

First, use a meeting agenda for every meeting. Include the normal items like the name of the meeting group, the day and date of the meeting, the start and stop times for the meeting, and a list of agenda items. Refine the agenda item list by including a time for each topic and an indication of who is responsible for the topic discussion. Then add a column that indicates topic by topic whether an information-only presentation is going to be made, a discussion is going to occur, or whether a decision is needed. Adding these details to the agenda items encourages people to prepare for the meeting and to come ready to make a decision when it is needed.

Next, talk individually to contributors. Communicate to each person invited to the meeting why they are needed and what role they have in presenting information and in making the decisions expected to be made at the meeting. Share the agenda during this in-person conversation and ask whether anything else needs to be added to the agenda to ensure a decision gets made in the meeting. Finally, if you are the authorized decision maker, *be at the meeting.* When you can't make the meeting, let others know so that the meeting can be cancelled, or so that directions can be given to the team about their role in making a decision recommendation or about their now-given authority to make the current decision.

Finally, remember that decisions must result in action. People want to know what action to take to accomplish their work objectives. Improve decision making and workplace results also improve. Whether using command-and-control decision making or reaching consensus on a decision, action must follow.

While working for a privately held company that produced training material, I once attended an executive meeting on behalf of my boss. After the meeting I asked her whether each team member knew by some internal meeting code what was to be done as a result of each meeting. I thought that I had missed the cues and that surely there was an assignment-giving sequence that had happened without my recognizing it. Instead, my boss said, "No, we never get clear assignments at the end of meetings." This book's premise includes that making decisions leads to decision implementation that improves the level and quality of work getting done.

The Importance of Consensus

Consensus is important enough to include in newspaper headlines. Discussions of collaboration and building consensus arise in surprising places including obituaries, advertising, and news items tied to business transactions. Businesses selling their services to others often make mention of consensus and collaboration in their advertisements. For instance, Toshiba ads in 2007 included these phrases: "Two superpowers join forces," and "Bring two opposing forces together to work for you." Another example comes from Capgemini's 2007 campaign that included the phrase and product-name coinage "Collaborative Business Experience" for their services offering. The biotech and pharmaceutical industries ran a special advertising section in the March 6, 2007, edition of *The Wall Street Journal* that began with "Corporate Collaboration Creates New Opportunities." And consensus is valued enough that it was included in an Idaho obituary for "Colleague and past Director of the Idaho Commission on the Arts." Dan Harpole's obituary mentioned "his talent for consensus." After mentioning his battle with cancer and his early passing from this life, and in addition to the long list of his professional and family accomplishments, a paragraph from his obituary reads:

> Dan thrived on the lives and challenges around him—on what is now called "networking." His attitude and leadership led to a legacy of accomplishments on behalf of the arts in Idaho. Not a little of it was his talent for consensus or accord, which he once

attributed to being the seventh of ten children: "When you're in a big family, you learn to negotiate for your life," he quipped.

Notice that this obituary paragraph includes many of the elements involved in coming to consensus. "Negotiation" is often a needed process in reaching consensus. "Accord" is another way to describe agreement. The size of a decision-making group is referenced in the phrase "being the seventh of ten children." The size of a decision group matters to the timing and process of reaching consensus because, the larger the group, the more time it takes to reach consensus. The fact that consensus building was one of Dan's hallmark behaviors and that it was mentioned in his obituary proves that the skill set matters and is worthy of being remembered because its effective use is so often lacking in today's leaders and teams.

Collaboration, Consensus, Cooperation, and Command and Control

For the *Moving Out of the Box* decision-making discussions, Merriam-Webster's Collegiate® Dictionary, Eleventh Edition©2007 definitions are used by permission from Merriam-Webster Inc. (www.Merriam-Webster.com) and are presented in italics below. Notice that the variations in the definitions provide the nuances of meaning that lead to the five ChoiceMark stages, levels of consensus, and decision profiles. Also notice that the word consensus is not a verb, which means that as a noun, consensus results from and requires other actions (verbs) to be taken before consensus can be reached. Consent is the root word and is the verb that describes the act of giving approval or of agreeing to something.

The definitions:

> *Consensus—noun 1.a. general agreement: unanimity b. the judgment arrived at by most of those concerned 2. group solidarity in sentiment and belief.*

Embedded in these three definitions are the ChoiceMarks stages of consensus: extreme excitement, which correlates to "unanimity"; engaged enthusiasm, which correlates to definition 1.b.; and neutral, which can correlate to definition 2 because when no one blocks a decision, work can still proceed. Some dictionaries expand the definition of consensus to the point that all five ChoiceMark stages of consensus are described. In current use, consensus decision making focuses on the process or manner of decision making in which everyone has a say or offers input before everyone or nearly everyone agrees to a decision.

Next is the root word of consensus: consent.

> *Consent—verb 1. to give assent or approval: agree*
> *Consent—noun 1. compliance in or approval of what is done or proposed by another: Acquiescence 2. agreement as to action or opinion; specifically: voluntary agreement by a people to organize a civil society and give authority to the government.*

Consent is often used in formal and governmental meetings to describe "consent agendas," which are used when a series of topics or decisions have been discussed already and are awaiting final approval for action to then occur. The phrases "to give consent" or "to be consenting" are often used in adult, parental, and social roles and discussions. The *Moving Out of the Box* discussion uses consent as one process for reaching consensus or for making a decision. And, the reach-consensus skill set supports and contributes to the activities of collaboration and cooperation. Both collaboration and cooperation additionally require such skill sets as listening, networking, resource exploration and procurement, partnering, and communication.

Next are the definitions for words that are often used interchangeably with consensus: collaboration and collaborate. However, you'll see that collaboration is not consensus but that collaboration implies that as a result of working jointly with others some level of consensus must have been reached in order for the group to move forward. And in the second definition of collaborate, more of the command-and-control arena of leading and decision making is implied.

> *Collaboration—noun—the act of or result from collaborating.*
> *Collaborate—verb—1. to work jointly with others or together especially in an intellectual endeavor 2. to cooperate with or willingly assist an enemy of one's country and especially an occupying force 3. to cooperate with an agency or instrumentality with which one is not immediately connected.*

The first and third definitions for collaborate are the ones typically used in business settings. The second definition for collaborate is most often heard in government or military settings where command-and-control decision making is used.

Do you work in a command-and-control decision environment—one in which orders or requests are issued from higher in the organization and somewhere lower in the organization implementation must occur? Or, do you work in a corporate culture where the goal is to be nice, even at the expense of workplace productivity, safety, and morale? And is this nice culture focused on collaboration or consensus as the primary decision process? Over the years, I have worked with one high-technology company and one nonprofit that each had a culture of "consensus nice." Here's what a culture of "consensus nice" includes: getting input from everyone, smiling in agreement in meetings, and then often after the meeting complaining about a decision made, even to the point of undermining it. A "consensus nice" culture also includes believing so much in the potential of people that even when performance problems occur, rather than confronting the poor performance and offering skill-building opportunities, the problems are not mentioned. The poor-performing employees are then either left in place poisoning those who work with and for them or are moved to another division of the company without any coaching or warning being given to the new employer division. Corporate cultures of "consensus nice" are really operating in anti-survival mode because individuals are not committing to action at the level required for improved implementation to occur and the whole organization ends up suffering.

Another word heard in consensus discussions is "cooperate." Typical phrases include: "Let's cooperate to get this done," or, "How about some cooperation here?"

The definitions for cooperation and cooperate include "acting with others for a common effort" and yet this does not directly connect to "consensus."

> *Cooperation—noun—1. the action of cooperating: common effort 2. association of persons for common benefit.*
>
> *Cooperate—verb—1. to act with another or others: act together or in compliance 2. to associate with another or others for mutual benefit.*

Notice that consensus, collaboration, and cooperation are nouns. The importance of this is that each is the result of process actions and verbs such as consent, collaborate, cooperate, negotiate, work, act, and associate. Next, notice that the words command and control are both nouns and verbs, both results and processes. This is worth noting because *Moving Out of the Box* suggests that both process (the manner in which a decision is made) and the final result are important for best-possible decision making to occur and to be followed by implementation.

The phrase and practice of " command-and-control" decision making has been around for centuries. Command and control is heard today in such settings as the military, law enforcement, governmental decision-making bodies, and in hierarchical organizations focused on centralized decision making. Here are the word definitions:

> *Command—verb—1. to direct authoritatively: Order 2. to exercise a dominating influence over: have command of;*
>
> *and as an intransitive verb—1. to have or exercise direct authority: govern. 2. to give orders 3. to be commander. 4. to dominate as if from an elevated place.*
>
> *Command—noun 1.a. an order given b. a signal that actuates a device 2.a. the ability to control: mastery b. the authority or right to command c. the power to dominate 3. the act of commanding 4. the personnel, area, or organization under a commander 5. a position of highest usually military authority. Syn: Power*
>
> *Control—verb—1.a. archaic definition—to check, test, or verify by evidence or experiments 1.b. to incorporate suitable controls in 2.a. to exercise retraining or directing influence over: regulate 2.b. to have power over: rule 2.c. to reduce the incidence or severity of especially innocuous levels.*
>
> *Control—noun—1.a. an act or instance of controlling; also: power or authority to guide or manage b. skill in the use of a tool, instrument, technique or artistic medium c. the regulation of economic activity especially by government directive d. the ability of a baseball pitcher to control the location of a pitch within the strike zone 2. restraint, reserve 3. one that controls. Syn. Power*

Command and control seem harsh, hierarchical, and nonnegotiable and list the same synonym: power. Yet, command-and-control decision making is critical when time is of the essence and a clear communication system is needed. Command and control is characterized by such phrases as "one person is in charge," "we do what we are told," and "there is a chain of command that we follow." Collaborate and cooperate seem soft and negotiable, and respectively list each other in their lists of synonyms. Consent carries the implication that discussion occurred and a voluntarily given level of agreement was reached. Consent lists "agreement" as its synonym. The actions of collaborating and coming to consensus also have characteristic phrases such as: "We all talked about it and agreed to our decision," "We gathered input from everyone before we reached a decision," and "Everyone seemed happy with the decision and willing to move forward." The word consensus continues to stand somewhat alone by definition because it is the result of such processes as discussion, debate, information gathering, brainstorming, and decision making.

Further differences between command-and-control decision making and consensus-driven decision making illustrate when each decision approach is best to use. Command-and-control decision making can happen in an instant. Decisions made in an instant sometimes fail to include the quantity of detailed information needed to make best-possible long-term decisions. However, the nature of effective command-and-control decision making is that an immediate decision and action-implementation strategy is needed. When time is less of an issue, a more time-consuming approach to decision making can occur. Coming to consensus requires more discussion and more time. Collaborative- and consensus-driven decision making requires time, multiple inputs, discussion, and decision making followed by implementation actions. Volumes of relevant and accurate information can be sought before decisions are made.

This is where the power of the five stages and mindsets of the ChoiceMarks tool presented in this book come into play. Using ChoiceMarks during decision discussions helps to expand the discussions, enlarge debate, and invite multiple inputs in order for best-possible decision making to occur in both consensus-driven and command-and-control decision making. In the chapters ahead, you'll discover five consensus-oriented decision-making profiles and stages, none necessarily better than any other. You'll also discover how to steer your group into the most effective profile or stage of consensus. The five ChoiceMarks consensus stages and profiles are

- **Anti-Survival.** The nay-sayers have control. And sometimes they should be listened to.

- **Boxed-in.** When no one can come up with fresh ideas, it's time to think out of the box.

- **Neutral.** Nobody terribly excited or negative? Don't worry, sometimes this isn't a bad place to be to make a good decision.

- **Engaged Enthusiasm.** If you can get the team into this state of being, chances are that a good decision will result.

- **Extreme Excitement.** Most team leaders think this is where the team needs to be to make a good decision. It's nice, but not required.

These are the five levels or stages of agreement that can be reached through a consensus-oriented process. Two levels bring further action to a halt: anti-survival and boxed-in. Two levels allow action to proceed: engaged enthusiasm and extreme excitement. And the fifth level of agreement or consensus can flip-flop, waffle, or vacillate depending on the ChoiceMarks profile of the person who is in neutral (you'll learn more about this in Chapter 2). All in all, *Moving Out of the Box* will help improve group and individual communication, problem solving, decision making, and decision implementation, regardless of the task at hand.

Making Decisions More Easily

To come to consensus or to reach agreement on how to proceed, groups need tools for the discussion that leads up to reaching consensus. Discussion tools include problem solving, brainstorming, dialogues, appreciative inquiry, pros and cons, scattergrams, flowcharts, project management lists, timelines, and more. The use of these discussion tools ultimately needs to lead to decision making. Otherwise individuals and groups sit and spin in inaction, miss critical deadlines, and ultimately fail to accomplish the tasks and mission at hand.

One poorly made decision can be recovered from. Two poorly made decisions are more difficult to recover from. And of course, the more poor decision making that happens, the more difficult it is to change the decision-making pattern, to recover, and to re-learn how to make good decisions. Inaction is a decision. Action is a decision. What kind of action to take is a decision. "Who is going to do what by when?" is a series of decisions.

Decisions can be demanded. Decisions also can be invited. Command-and-control decision environments lean toward demanding decisions. Consensus-driven environments lean toward inviting input and agreed upon decisions. An example of inviting input comes from a public library reference desk. While asking a research question, I came across the library's suggestion box headline, "Exclaim Yourself." This creative invitation is meant to elicit comments about the library, its services, and its resources. In the workplace at large, the "explain yourself" phrase is usually a demand that puts people into defensive modes of interacting. Instead, reframe the demand into an invitation or an inviting question delivered in a tone of voice that creates a willingness to provide input on the part of all team members. Hold the decision discussion using the ChoiceMarks to reach a best-possible decision. Then gain action commitments in order to ensure that follow-up actions and implementation occurs. Use the checklist that follows to build better decision-making environments.

A Checklist for Making Decisions Easier to Make

1. Establish rules for the decision-making process. Decision-making rules guide debate, discussion, and information gathering. However, the rules themselves do not lead to final decisions. These rules are the guidelines for interactions that lead more successfully to best-possible decisions. Decision-making rules include the following.

Begin with team or group agreement on what communication rules will be used during consensus-driven decision making. For instance, "We'll listen to each other without interrupting," or, "We'll share our expertise rather than withholding it." Some teams even include, "We'll come to meetings on time and prepared to give input and make decisions." Next, commit to preparing an agenda and distributing it before each meeting. Effective agenda inclusions were outlined earlier in this chapter. Then, agree on meeting-room tools such as flipcharts or technology boards for recording key ideas and action items. The use of shared technology tools also should be agreed upon for consistent use in meetings.

Now for the roles that can be performed in every meeting. Agree on which of these roles will be used in each decision-making meeting. Of course, there will be a clearly named meeting facilitator or meeting leader who is responsible for accomplishing the agenda in a timely manner while gathering input from participants and maintaining team willingness to work together to make decisions and get things done. Next is the recording secretary for the meeting. The secretary is responsible for producing meeting minutes that include the name of the meeting group, the date of the meeting, the meeting attendees, an overview of discussions held and information shared, and most importantly the decision list that includes who is going to do what by when. The third meeting role is that of timekeeper, a person who lets both the meeting leader and participants know when topic times are half consumed and when the topic end times have been reached. Timekeeping helps focus discussions and keep them moving forward. Other meeting roles include: gatekeeper, one who makes sure everyone gets a chance to speak up and be heard; participants, those without whom the meeting is not needed and an email could have been sent instead; and sometimes a devil's advocate, one who will offer opposing points of view when the group wants to be sure that these are expressed during a discussion.

Process agreements are also a part of up-front agreement setting. During these agreements, the team decides on which of the following or which combinations of the following will be put into practice. Robert's Rules of Order and making motions can be used in command-and-control style decision-making environments. Choice-Marks are more often used in consensus-oriented decision environments. Brainstorming, idea generation, and problem-solving models can be used in both decision environments. And voting is an intermediary process when time pressures force a consensus-oriented discussion to reach a quick conclusion or when enough discussion has happened in a command-and-control discussion sequence.

2. Agree to reach a decision. Many groups leave discussions without a clear decision. Agree to make a decision. Use the ChoiceMarks to expand discussions, uncover challenges or barriers, and to reach best-possible decisions. Summarize the decisions and assignments made before the discussion or meeting ends.

3. Take action, implement the decision. Decisions made without implementation are a waste of time, energy and resources. And decisions made with no resulting implementation are worthless when it comes to getting things done for the larger good of an organization and the fulfillment of its mission. Once a decision is made action must follow.

4. When stuck, get unstuck and make a decision. Use the ChoiceMarks to reopen and enlarge the conversation in order to reach best-possible decisions.

5. Recognize that individual thinking styles affect the decision-making process. Every person in a decision discussion has a different focus or worldview: task focus; relationship focus; reactive versus reflective approaches; right brain-creative versus left brain-logical approaches; optimistic versus pessimistic; and other focal point combinations. Life experiences that affect individual thinking and problem solving approaches come into play when people make decisions too. We all carry stories about ourselves, our work, and our co-workers. The stories we hold onto and believe in provide a part of our base for making decisions. In Chapter 2, we explore further the consensus, waffling or indecisive, and command-and-control decision-making styles that people naturally gravitate toward when making decisions.

Chapter Summary

Every day is a choice. What are you choosing?

If you are choosing to let others run your life, or sitting quietly by as others debate action and decisions, today is your opportunity to acquire skills for entering the debate in ways that your point of view gets heard. If you are pushing others to arrive at decisions they are uncomfortable with and not seeing the implementation successes you'd hoped for, today is your opportunity to learn how to listen more carefully to the available information and experience that can be used to improve decision making and results. This book is about command and control and the ChoiceMarks tool for conversation and decision making that allows best-possible decisions to be made every time a decision needs to be made. In the chapters ahead you'll learn how teams and team leaders can improve communication, make better decisions, and reach goals more effectively, quickly, and productively. The move-out-of-the-box approach to making decisions is about being invigorated, open minded, and action oriented so that best-possible decision making occurs.

CHAPTER 2

Equal Decision-Making Processes: Command-and-Control and Collaborative Consensus

The Battle Is On

Tired of being bossed around and told to go to war, young adults moving into the workforce in the 1960s and 1970s began the push-back against the command-and-control culture of government, education, and society. By the late 1980s and early 1990s, the either-or battle between command-and-control and consensus-driven decision making began in full. The push for improved quality, increased productivity, greater efficiencies, and larger profit margins caused organizations to try approaches other than command-and-control for gaining the improvements. Hoping to empower people at all parts of an organization, the "come to consensus," "cross-train team members," and "do things in teams" approaches moved into organizations of all sizes. At the same time, the command-and-control style of leading change was seen in the downsizing and rightsizing movement. Then open-book management, coming from the consensus side of the battle, came onto the scene by the end of the century.

Nearly two decades later, the results of the battle have ranged from productive team-driven decisions and results to paralyzed team members unwilling to take the risks involved with decision making; and from well-followed decision implementations to disastrous breakdowns of communication systems during emergencies. Whenever results were (and are) less than expected, it was due to failures at many levels. Rather than diving into all of them here, which would require an historic analysis larger than the scope of this book, I'll focus on the primary elements that cause individuals and groups to get stuck when making decisions.

The first reason comes from the complaint I hear most often in working with clients focused on improving their meetings and their decision-making ability: "The right people with the authority to make the decision aren't in the room." Further research has uncovered that one of two things are happening when this complaint is heard. Either the people with organizational authority are not in the room during decision-making discussions, or the organization has not clearly communicated to the team that it as a group has the authority to make decisions. Saying that a team needs to make decisions but not giving a team the authority to act or spend money leaves the team unable and unwilling to make real decisions. Also uncovered, and yet not surprising, is that an unwillingness to take risks is another reason groups fail to make decisions. With the move to consensus-driven decisions, less people are willing to take risks for fear of looking bad, getting demoted, project failure, or even of getting fired if things go poorly.

A third reason teams are now allegedly getting stuck is the old phrase "all talk and no action." This phrase is often used to describe people who have grand ideas but never act on them, or who tell great stories of what they'll do and then don't do it. Because coming to consensus requires more discussion time than a command-and-control approach to making decisions, people who prefer command-style decisions are prone to viewing coming to consensus as "all talk and no action." In team-focused organizations across all sectors, the frustration over more hours in meetings with a sense of less overall workplace productivity has spawned an entire facilitation industry that focuses on leading productive meetings for those who are not being successful on their own. This points out the need for individuals in organizations to master a variety of group process and decision-making tools.

Add to the first three reasons teams are getting stuck two areas seldom identified by teams and organizations. These two areas contribute to trouble making decisions and yet they are very real dimensions of the dilemma of being stuck: timing and the lack of having the right people with the right expertise present to give input during the meeting. The timing dimension cuts two ways: when more time is available than seems to be needed, decisions get put off; and when a decision seems rushed, people then to hesitate and even prevent themselves from making a decision when one is desperately needed. Missing expertise can affect the timely ability of a group to make a decision. When the people with the needed expertise aren't at the decision-making discussion, a decision may not get made, a best-possible decision may not get made, or the decision that gets made doesn't end up having the commitment to action needed for the decision to be implemented. Finally, I'll offer that the biggest reason groups get stuck when making decisions is that individuals have not mastered a variety of decision-making approaches and tools. *Moving Out of the Box* of course focuses on this cause for groups getting stuck and provides a new point of view— "command-and-control and consensus driven are equal decision-making tools"— along with a presentation of a new ChoiceMarks tool for reaching consensus.

Dozens of decision-making approaches, styles, and tools exist. *Moving Out of the Box* focuses on the command-and-control and consensus approaches to making decisions because they have become the nemesis and antithesis of each other when they don't have to be. They are simply two tools for making decisions. They are appropriate in different situations and they can be used in tandem in some situations. The two surveys in this chapter help you to identify your preferred decision-making style and then to define your preferred approach and mindset when working with a consensus-driven approach to making decisions.

Identify Your Preferred Decision-Making Style: The Decision Style Survey

In each of the ten boxes below, circle the sentence that best describes how you make decisions.

Box 1

A. Once the team makes a decision, I'm willing to help implement it.

B. Once I make a decision, I start questioning whether it was the right decision.

C. Once I make a decision, I'm done.

Box 2

A. When the team makes a decision I'm not in agreement with, I speak up.

B. When the team makes a decision I'm not in agreement with, I generally don't say anything.

C. When the team makes a decision I'm not in agreement with, I may speak against it but I don't commit to any implementation actions.

Box 3

A. During discussions, I want to share my ideas and hear from everyone else too.

B. During discussions, I focus on listening to everyone else.

C. During discussions, I often find myself getting impatient with all the talk.

Box 4

A. Unless we hear from everyone, we should not make a decision.

B. Sometimes I just don't care and want to leave the room.

C. When we don't reach a decision, my time has been wasted.

Box 5

A. Once we have heard from everyone, we can make a decision.

B. Once we listen to all ideas, spend more time to gather final data related to all of the ideas, and then have a final discussion on everything, then we can make a decision.

C. Once we've hit the critical details, then a decision can be made.

Box 6

A. When there is disagreement, we should find out where the problems are, talk them through and reach a decision together.

B. When there is disagreement, we should identify what additional information we need and then come back to the table for discussion.

C. When there is disagreement, someone needs to make a decision so we can move ahead.

Box 7

A. When deadlines are upon us, we should still take time to get everyone's input before making a decision.

B. When deadlines are upon us, we should get input and then someone needs to tell us what needs to be done by when.

C. When deadlines are upon us, someone should say what needs to be done by when.

Box 8

A. When implementing our decision, we should keep talking to each other to achieve our goal.

B. When implementing our decision, we should get the work done, talking to each other as needed in case new decisions need to be reached along the way.

C. When implementing our decision, everyone should get their work done and report back on any problems.

Box 9

A. While implementing our decision, I know who to contact to get input or help to get things done.

B. While implementing decisions, I usually get my part done and don't always know who can help get things done.

C. While implementing a decision, I get my part done.

Box 10

A. When reviewing our accomplishments, we should each have an opportunity to talk about what worked, what didn't work, and what we need to do differently next time.

B. When reviewing our accomplishments, we should celebrate what went well.

C. When reviewing our accomplishments, we should be glad that we're done and move on to the next project.

SCORING DIRECTIONS

Below, record how many A, B, and C responses you had.

____ A—Consensus/Collaboration. Your decision-making preference is to involve others, secure buy-in before a decision is made, and to share both decision-making authority as well as responsibility for implementation. Taking time up front to involve people takes longer but you believe it is worth it.

____ B—Wafflers. On some occasions, waiting for more information or research helps to make better decisions. However, your decision-making preference is to not make a decision, and even to hope that someone else will make the decision so that you can take action based on their decision.

____ C—Command and Control. Your decision-making preference is to make a decision and move forward. Taking time to interact with others who may or may not have expertise seems like a waste of time to you.

Now, circle the decision-making personality above that has the highest point score total. This is the decision-making style that you tend to prefer and to rely on when participating in decision making. If you have a tied score, you tend to use these two approaches equally.

Notice that you may have a point total in all three of the styles. If the total score is fairly close in all three styles, consider that (a) you are a confident decision maker who knows when to use which decision-making approach, or (b) you are not really clear about when to use which decision-making style and you switch approaches so often that people aren't sure how you'll make a decision on any given day. Also notice that you may have a clear high-score decision-making style. If so, consider both the strengths and limitations of having a singular high point total. For instance, having a high point total for consensus/collaboration means that your strengths are gathering input from others, listening to multiple and even opposing points of view, and seeking general group agreements, and your potential limitations are not making decisions as quickly as they need to be made. Having a high point total for waffling means that your strength is being willing to wait out a decision-making cycle and your limitation is that others see you as permanently indecisive. Having a high point total for command and control means that your strengths are being decisive in a short time frame and your potential limitations are not getting enough information and being perceived as someone who doesn't listen to others.

The rest of this chapter will help you to strike a balance of decision-making styles.

Recognize Individual Decision-Making Styles

In addition to the strengths and potential limitations of the three main decision-making styles, pay attention to the characteristics and mindsets that help in the recognition of each style.

A. Consensus/Collaboration

This decision-making style is characterized by looking for input from others, wanting everyone or nearly everyone to be on-board with the decision, and working together as a team to get things done. This is the preferred environment of consensus-oriented decision makers. The "A" phrases from the above survey capture the essence and preferred approaches of consensus-and-collaboration-oriented decision makers. These phrases also are often the mindsets of people working from a consensus style of decision making.

- Once the team makes a decision, I'm willing to help implement it.
- When the team makes a decision I'm not in agreement with, I speak up.
- During discussions, I want to share my ideas and hear from everyone else too.

- Unless we hear from everyone, we should not make a decision.
- Once we have heard from everyone, we can make a decision.
- When there is disagreement, we should find out where the problems are, talk them through, and reach a decision together.
- When deadlines are upon us, we should still take time to get everyone's input before making a decision.
- When implementing our decision, we should keep talking to each other to achieve our goal.
- While implementing our decision, I know who to contact to get input or help to get things done.
- When reviewing our accomplishments, we should each have an opportunity to talk about what worked, what didn't work, and what we need to do differently next time.

B. Wafflers

This decision-making style is characterized by being indecisive throughout and after a decision-making event. Wafflers lose energy and time by constantly debating what the right or best decision is. You'll recognize the "B" phrases from the above survey as things wafflers say. These phrases also are often the mindsets of people working in waffler mode.

- Once I make a decision, I start questioning whether it was the right decision.
- When the team makes a decision I'm not in agreement with, I generally don't say anything.
- During discussions, I focus on listening to everyone else.
- Once we listen to all ideas, spend more time to gather final data related to all of the ideas, and then have a final discussion on everything, then we can make a decision.
- Sometimes I just don't care and want to leave the room.
- When there is disagreement, we should identify what additional information we need and then come back to the table for discussion.
- When deadlines are upon us, we should get input and then someone needs to tell us what needs to be done by when.
- When implementing our decision, we should get the work done, talking to each other as needed in case new decisions need to be reached along the way.
- While implementing decisions, I usually get my part done and don't always know who can help get things done.
- When reviewing our accomplishments, we should celebrate what went well.

C. Command and Control

This decision-making style is characterized by always being ready for a decision to be made, an assignment to be given, and action to be taken. It is almost a state of being and living for the command-and-control decision maker. You'll recognize the

"C" phrases and mindsets from the above survey as signals that you are dealing with someone who lives in a command-and-control decision-making environment.

- Once I make a decision, I'm done.
- When the team makes a decision I'm not in agreement with, I may speak against it but I don't commit to any implementation actions.
- During discussions, I often find myself getting impatient with all the talk.
- When we don't reach a decision, my time has been wasted.
- Once we've hit the critical details, then a decision can be made.
- When there is disagreement, someone needs to make a decision so we can move ahead.
- When deadlines are upon us, someone should say what needs to be done by when.
- When implementing our decision, everyone should get their work done and report back on any problems.
- While implementing a decision, I get my part done.
- When reviewing our accomplishments, we should be glad that we're done and move on to the next project.

Why Consensus and Command-and-Control Decision Making are Equally Effective

As stated earlier in the chapter, coming to consensus and command and control are tools for decision making. Here are seven supporting statements for this book's premise that they are equally useful tools.

First, different situations demand different approaches. We've all learned this over the years in our professional and in our personal lives.

Second, emergency situations require immediate take-charge decision making and instruction giving. In emergencies, time is of the essence making a command-and-control style of decision appropriate.

Third, people are looking for leaders. At the end of any decision-making process, a clear decision needs to be made and include clear assignments of the work that needs to be done. In other words, whatever tool you choose to use, be sure the decision and resulting actions are clear to all involved.

Fourth, the closeness of a deadline can dictate which style of decision making is best to implement. When time is short or a decision is urgent, a command-and-control approach is appropriate. When more time is available to gain input and buy-in and the decision itself can be scheduled into a timeline, a consensus approach is appropriate.

Fifth, a supporting statement which has entered the scene during the last decade, more regulatory agencies are requiring consensus and input before final decisions are to be made. For instance, federal and state transportation dollars for roads often include having neighborhood and community-wide meetings before and during the planning and approval processes.

Supporting statements six and seven provide a comparison and contrast of sorts on when to use which approach.

Sixth, consensus-driven decisions can be made when the right people with the right expertise and authority are at the table and have a flexible deadline in making a decision. A lack of given authority for making decisions undermines a consensus approach. And, if the right people aren't present, opt to cancel the meeting; make assignments and reconvene to make a decision; or discuss details now and make a recommendation to the person(s) with authority.

And seventh, command-and-control decisions can be made when the person or people with the right authority are present and the timing is now. When no clear authority exists and yet a decision is demanded due to urgency, someone must take control, make decisions, and deal with the authority issue in the aftermath of the situation. As you can see, there is a situation-appropriate time for both decision-making approaches.

How the Decision-Making Styles Handle Conflict

Each decision-making style has a different approach to handling conflict. It is important to recognize this when working through a decision-making process. Otherwise, much needed input may not be given because the conflict exists, poorly made decisions result, and even poor implementation can occur. The consensus approach wants to avoid conflict and gain buy-in. By talking everything through with everyone, the goal is to reach agreement with as little conflict as possible. The waffler approach wants to avoid conflict and will even leave the room to avoid it. The command-and-control approach wants to get a decision made even if there is conflict. To reach a decision even when there is conflict, the best overall approach is to turn to the ChoiceMarks for improving the discussion and moving to a decision. Specifically, each decision-making approach used by individuals or an entire team will need the following things when a conflict arises and a decision needs to be made.

When there's a conflict, both consensus-driven and waffler-leaning decision makers need an opportunity to talk things through, to gather more information, and to explore what options may work best. If the conflict becomes too great, the team leader may need to have one-on-one meetings with team members in order to discover what the conflict stems from and gather ideas about how the team can move forward to reach a decision. If the conflict prevails and a decision that has not been reached yet is still needed, sometimes it becomes necessary to shift into a command-and-control approach to reach a decision and assign action items for implementation.

When command-and-control-driven decision makers and teams are in conflict, the scene can sometimes look like a battle of wills. As a result, command-and-control decision making that reaches any level of conflict is best served by a summary statement of the problem, a brief discussion of the options, and the consequences or results of choosing individual options and then guidance to a decision. If a decision still cannot be reached, it is time to restate the authority for decision making and to have the person or people "in charge" make the decision.

Move Past Stuck

Synergy has been a business watchword for nearly three decades. Just like consensus, sometimes it works. And other times the promised synergy from divergent product lines or even matched product lines from parent companies with divergent cultures never comes to fruition—proof that clear plans and objectives can stall or get stuck, forcing new decisions to be made. The challenges and frustrations that arise from stalled or stuck decision making can lead to conflict. However, with a mastery of the ChoiceMarks consensus tools, destructive conflict can be avoided, stuck spots can be worked through, and decisions can be reached. ChoiceMarks invite discussion when a group is stuck. They also provide questions to ask in order to expand and enlarge conversations so best-possible decision making can be made. The following ChoiceMarks Profile will help you identify your own preferences for approaching decision discussions.

The ChoiceMarks Profile: Identify your Decision— Discussion Approach

Directions: In each of the five question blocks that follow, rank the statements in order of their seeming most like you. Ranking an item "1" means it is MOST like you. Ranking an item "5" means it is LEAST like you. Be sure to use each rank only once in each box.

Example:

Question A   Rank

1. I prefer not to participate in teams.   __4__

2. I prefer to contribute a devil's advocate position during discussions.   __5__

3. I prefer to listen during discussions.   __3__

4. I prefer to engage in conversations and share my expertise.   __2__

5. I prefer being excited about discussions and getting others to   __1__
   participate.

ChoiceMarks Profile

Question A   Rank

1. I prefer not to participate in teams.   ____

2. I prefer to contribute a devil's advocate position during discussions. ____

3. I prefer to listen during discussions. ____

4. I prefer to engage in conversations and share my expertise. ____

5. I prefer being excited about discussions and getting others to participate. ____

Question B

1. I tend to see problems before others do. ____

2. I tend to know what has and hasn't worked. ____

3. I tend to want more information before making decisions. ____

4. I tend to see solutions before others do. ____

5. I tend to encourage others to participate in implementation. ____

Question C

1. Others tell me to "stop being so negative all of the time." ____

2. Others tell me to "get out of my box and help find a solution." ____

3. Others tell me to "take a position." ____

4. Others tell me "go ahead without me, you don't need me at this point." ____

5. Others tell me "stop being so excited all the time." ____

Question D

1. After some decisions, others have come to me and said ____
   "We should have listened, some of your reasons for not doing this were right."

2. After some decisions, others have come to me and said ____
   "Several of your experiences happened again to us."

3. After some decisions, others have come to me and said   _____
             "What do you think about how things turned out?"

4. After some decisions, others have come to me and said   _____
             "Your persistence paid off, things got done."

5. After some decisions, others have come to me and said   _____
             "Your excitement sure pulled this project off. Without it we might not
                    have succeeded."

Question E

1. I wish people wouldn't take so many risks without considering the consequences.   _____

2. I wish people would listen to my experience.   _____

3. I wish people would actively ask for my input.   _____

4. I wish people would more actively engage in our decision discussions.   _____

5. I wish people would focus on the good aspects, get committed, and   _____
join the team's "yes" decision.

SCORING DIRECTIONS

To discover your ChoiceMarks Profile, add your ranking scores together, one question at a time.

Question

A. Ranking Point Total _____   The ChoiceMark Profile is Anti-Survival.

B. Ranking Point Total _____   The ChoiceMark Profile is Boxed-In.

C. Ranking Point Total _____   The ChoiceMark Profile is Neutral.

D. Ranking Point Total _____   The ChoiceMark Profile is Engaged Enthusiasm.

E. Ranking Point Total _____   The ChoiceMark Profile is Extreme Excitement.

Note that ranking point totals less than 5 or greater than 25 are not possible, so check your rankings and add your totals again if this occurs. Also notice that you may have one ChoiceMark Profile that has a clearly LOW point total. This is your predominate mindset when participating in discussions. If you have fairly close point totals, this means that you use multiple mindsets during discussions. And if you have a clearly HIGH point total, this is a mindset you rarely use during discussions. In Chapter 3 you'll learn more about each of the ChoiceMarks.

A Balance of the Two!

Across the United States, after experiencing poor communication channels post-natural disaster and during day-to-day cross-jurisdiction pursuits, law enforcement agencies are coming to consensus on how to work together so that their command-and-control protocols and decision structures can work more effectively across jurisdictions. System-wide decision making based on one jurisdiction, one experience, or one anecdote does not lead to best-possible decision making. While serving two years in Idaho's legislature, I was surprised at the number of times that decisions were made based on stories, anecdotes, and a singular experience from as far back as 50 years ago. One anecdote does not lead to good group decision making. Of course, we each hold dear the stories that inform and influence our decision making. Yet, when we fail to listen to others, we've failed to gather relevant information that can lead to better decision making. One story is just that, one story. More information, experience, data, and scenario results are needed to be parts of decision-making discussions. Business, nonprofit, and governmental decisions need data and experience on the discussion table so that best-possible decisions are made.

Also, while serving in Idaho's House of Representatives, I met two-star General Jim Brooks. We served together on a regional transportation committee that worked on legislation to present during the 2007 Idaho session. What struck me about General Brooks is that while he comes from a four-decade service history with the U.S. military and command-and-control environments, his committee comments made clear that he also had a firm grounding in and mastery of collaborative approaches and consensus-driven decision making. I had the good fortune to meet at length with General Brooks to gather his thoughts on the need for both command-and-control and consensus-oriented decision making.

By way of background, General Jim Brooks served 42 years in uniform beginning as a commissioned officer in the U.S. Army during World War II, serving in a variety of positions and holding a flying status for 35 years. He ultimately retired after 10 years as Commander of the Idaho National Guard. Over the years, General Brooks also worked for five Idaho governors and on five presidentially declared disasters. Brooks was responsible for presenting the Military Division's budget and other legislative initiatives to the legislature every year from 1953 to 1985. In addition to a successful service career and decades of volunteerism, General Brooks has been married, to the same wife he notes, for 60 years.

What follows is an abbreviated interview with General Brooks about balancing the use of command-and-control decisions and consensus-driven decision making.

General Brooks: Unlike the older regular military service, the Guard is and always has been a volunteer service. Subject to the traditional military hierarchy and culture of command and control yes, but from a realistic standpoint a quasi-civilian organization that requires practical as well as authoritative leadership. In short, there is no real penalty to apply if members simply quit and go home because they don't like the leadership and policies adopted. So, the challenge is to "mix" the command and consensus styles of management in order to lead from the middle to accomplish anything at all. "Power" is most effective when it doesn't have to be used. Also, I have found that the majority of folks are basically followers, almost crying out for leadership and will accept direction that is perceived to be reasonable and positive even if slanted on the dictatorial (the definition of benevolent dictatorship). The military is often perceived as little more than soldiers in combat gear on mammoth vehicles bristling with guns as seen on TV. This is partly true but the challenge for leadership goes much further. The art of effective management of people, dollars, and things is what brings success.

Kemp: When have you seen command-and-control decision making work well?

General Brooks: In "emergency" or critical situations, military or otherwise. Those affected really want someone to take charge and do something—now! In short, someone to take one step forward and say "follow me!" If the leader is trained (or experienced) in such situations and recognizes what needs to be done, people will follow. I had several such situations, the most challenging being June 5, 1976, when the Teton Dam in eastern Idaho failed. The Governor of Idaho put me in charge of coordinating state agencies and to act as the Governor's representative to federal agencies to deal with the aftermath. In emergency conditions, directions need to be given, now! There is no time for extended discussion or collaboration and consensus at the outset. People must be trained in how to solve problems, how to respond to the situation and how to relate to the media. Go to public officials and offer help. Don't wait for them to come to you. In an emergency, people are looking for direction. Identify who and where the influencers are so that things can get done. Good communication systems are needed though seldom available. You must have suggestions for elected officials because they still have the final decision-power for their cities and counties yet they typically don't have the resources or the expertise for handling the details of a disaster. Most of the public officials had little idea how to react but my organization was trained and did. The locals followed even though I had no legal authority over them.

General Brooks goes on to say that in order to deal with the multitude of decisions that must be made after a disaster or emergency has occurred, "You must know what should be done; lead the organization in that direction; and then others will line up to help too." In the Teton Dam's failure and the disaster conditions that existed in so many counties, Brooks offered suggestions, help, and resources to local officials that lead to solving their problems while state and federal agencies performed their emergency duties in a more command atmosphere. Locals with authority could then be in charge and make decisions based on the suggestions offered. This approach worked well and precluded the use of a full-on command-and-control style of disaster-addressing leadership. (Short of martial law or the failure to act, the ultimate authority of elected officials cannot be usurped.) The priority in handling an emergency must be to first save lives, establish communication systems including knowing who is where doing what and what communication technology is available. The next priority is to take care of human needs: find people; help them; provide medical help where needed; reconnect relatives; provide security, food, and shelter. Then focus on addressing the infrastructure needs.

After sharing this story, General Brooks offered this learning point:

General Brooks: If you don't know how to handle a specific situation or much about a specific subject, surround yourself with people who do and listen to them. The key, of course, is to determine what you need to know and then admit it when you don't. Sometimes ego can get in the way of this crucial practice. A significant crisis management challenge is also to determine when to withdraw the "command" atmosphere and transition to the typical "local" way of doing things—the environment the public is comfortable with.

Kemp: When have you seen consensus-oriented decision making work well?

General Brooks: In the Coalition for Public Transportation that I've served with you on. The challenge was how to get funding for public transportation. First, all the options were developed along with all the advantages and disadvantages of each and then presented/explained to the members of the coalition. Ample time was allowed for discussion and technical question-asking. The coalition membership was diverse. The staff behind the effort was knowledgeable and responsive to the members. The leaders were recognized as "honest" brokers and not simply involved because of a self-interest. The votes were democratic and while maybe not the first choice of some, the final action was acceptable. At least there was no minority report.   However, this form of decision making not only can consume eons of time it has several drawbacks—"Public" consensus can be very difficult to establish and the more people involved the more difficult it is. That's why the use of facilitators can be so valuable. Another common practice, and major problem, facing a consensus-driven decision is that of legal action. Those in dissent from almost any decision can be quick to turn to an attorney and the courts to settle the issue. One of the greatest weaknesses in today's method of solving problems legally is that judges are usually the least likely to know anything about the issue and case law is often nonexistent and in the process nothing at all gets done.

Kemp: You mentioned "minority reports." When have you seen minority reports work well?

General Brooks: Minority reports: put concerns into the record of a meeting and decision-making sequence yet generally don't change decisions. Committees, boards, legislative committees, task forces, and teams can all use minority reports to voice concern, particularly when the final vote is close. Minority reports made in governmental processes are apt to make the press if there is a hint of controversy.

Author note: And in corporate settings there may be a legal affect or impact of having filed a minority report.

Kemp: Which decision-making approach do you believe works best? Is it situational?

General Brooks: Yes it is situational. The "easy" way is probably to follow the command system but that can lead to major complications later. There is also an inherent danger in the exercise of authoritative action. When the smoke clears many of those that you thought were with you might be found looking out the window when it's time to explain why things happened as they did.

Kemp: I propose that we need commanding collaborators in chief because of the premise that both decision approaches are valid. What do you think would happen if we had CEOs, governors, and even a president that had equal facility with both command-and-control and consensus-driven decision-making approaches?

General Brooks: I think I would be all for it. It would take some very accomplished individuals to make it work. But it could work if the media would allow it (a whole other issue). The private sector at least has access to the "smart" folks that can be given and are the necessary command authority to sink or win in business. I would guess that the good ones already use both approaches assuming they are held accountable by their boards. That is if laws and regulations don't preclude it. But our governmental institutions are headed by political appointees and elected officials that are here today and gone tomorrow. Not that public servants are not accomplished and dedicated but generally there is little accountability for long-lasting decisions. And the buzz phrase "to run government like a business" is such a fallacy when most anyone who has been there knows that that is not possible. I honestly believe that government bureaucracy and today's legal system have all but strangled efficient management, of any type, particularly within the public sector.

Kemp: General, how did you learn to be a master of both command-and-control systems and collaborative consensus-driven decision systems?

General Brooks: The term "master" may be a bit strong but I had great mentors. One boss in particular modeled well the decision-making process and invested in my learning to make solid decisions too. In managing my team, I was available for collaboration but allowed the staff to do their jobs with the goal always being to make a decision as quickly as reasonable. After you've heard it all, move on to a decision for action or throw it away as a bad idea, or put it in the "too hard for now" box and move on to something else.

General Brooks had a personal staff of six members and an extended team staff of 40. When talking about power, General Brooks shares the following: "My staff knew their input was wanted and needed, and to keep it relevant. No game playing. Being intellectually honest was expected. Each member knew that they could be overruled because they knew I had the ultimate authority or power to approve or deny recommendations, make decisions and to get things done."

Kemp: When you talk about being intellectually honest, what do you mean?

General Brooks: To be intellectually honest means to voice an opinion, share information, have accurate data to support opinions, and to be 100 percent honest regardless of the fringe influence trying to make you stay quiet, or make you "say the right thing." Being intellectually honest includes not saying yes when it should be no. When your research says one thing, don't say another. Speak up with what needs to be heard rather than with what you think someone wants to hear. And don't cloud your meaning by adding terms of political correctness into your recommendations. Saying something you don't believe in is not intellectually honest nor is saying something politically correct that you don't believe in is intellectually honest.

Brooks goes on to say that he believes "being intellectually honest is perhaps the number one trait for a person in management and decision-making positions to have. Being honest with ourselves is very hard. And once a decision is made, help to pull it off. Don't work against it."

During our interview, I also had the opportunity to capture insightful decision-making snippets and recommendations, some of which you've read and others of which are in the chapters ahead. For instance, General Brooks says, "Over-scheduling prevents time for thinking, planning, and decision making. Today's hectic pacing and over-scheduling of people's time makes pausing long enough to make a decision difficult at best." Hurried and untrained thought prevents best-possible decision making. And this is when the ChoiceMarks are most needed in decision-making discussions. Working toward group consensus that leads to action is critical. Otherwise, the discussion has been all talk and idea generation without any decision regarding how to move forward and how to complete work more effectively. In Chapters 3 through 8, the ChoiceMarks consensus-driven decision-making tools are presented for you to add to your decision-making toolbox. In Chapter 9, this discussion is expanded into the effective use and implementation of command-and-control decision making along with consensus-driven decision approaches.

Chapter Summary

Consensus-driven decision makers would say, "Isn't this great information we're collecting? Let's keep reading and implement changes in our organization."

A waffler would say, "This seems interesting. Maybe we should learn more."

A command-and-control decision maker would say, "If you've already gotten what you need, stop reading. If not, read on."

And from the ChoiceMarks approach to decision making at this point in the *Moving Out of the Box* discussion, you might hear the following.

Anti-survival would say, "How will one more tool help us make decisions? Stop reading."

Boxed-in would say, "We've tried new tools before. They didn't work either, so you might as well stop reading."

Neutral would say, "Give this idea about the equality of decision-making tools a chance, keep reading."

Engaged enthusiasm would say, "The ChoiceMarks tool can give us a better way to have decision discussions and reach decisions. Keep reading so we can improve our decision culture."

And extreme excitement would say, "The surveys, profiles, and the interview in this chapter were really insightful. Won't it be great to be masters of both command-and-control and consensus-driven decision making?"

CHAPTER 3

ChoiceMarks Defined: Anti-Survival, Boxed-in, Neutral, Engaged Enthusiasm, Extreme Excitement

When meetings bog down, teams fall apart, and individuals decline to budge on their positions, it is time to implement the ChoiceMarks for decision making. As you read about in the preface, during a meeting I attended as a volunteer, I felt myself growing frustrated with the circles of conversation and lack of decision making that kept the group from moving forward. I noticed that questions were left unanswered, and needed questions went unasked. Some voiced frustrations while others left theirs unspoken. Exclamations and explanations were being bantered around the table. All the while, I observed that the meeting leader and the participants were struggling to make a decision and yet couldn't figure out how.

While in that 2002 volunteer meeting, I devised a set of decision-making tools based on what I'd learned over the years about decision making, coming to consensus, and getting groups stuck in the mode of not making decisions moving to make decisions. As I reflected on the situation, I realized that we already have question marks to seek out information, periods to say we've finished a thought, exclamation marks to add emphasis to a comment, commas to separate ideas, and quotation marks to show that someone is speaking or being quoted. So, where are the marks that tell us someone needs more information before a decision can be made, or tell us what kind of decision someone is leaning toward making? ChoiceMarks were born.

In addition to being styles of thinking (as we learned in Chapter 2), ChoiceMarks are decision-making tools that allow individuals and groups both to seek out more information to make a decision and to indicate where the decision is headed—*yes* or *no*. You can use ChoiceMarks to gather more information to determine when and on what you will move ahead. And the marks can be used to determine whether *yes* or *no* is the best response.

Think of ChoiceMarks as tools for thinking and decision making. You can use them by yourself to determine how you feel about the information you do have and to determine what additional information you need or want to make a decision. You also can use ChoiceMarks to sort out what information a group, team, or committee needs to make a decision and move forward to implement the decision.

When working with wafflers—people who never seem to make a decision—you can use ChoiceMarks to prompt a decision. And the next time a group is stuck waffling, use the ChoiceMarks to uncover where more information is needed for the whole group to reach a decision that allows the group to take action, make a commitment, and move on. Use ChoiceMarks to think more clearly and make decisions more easily. When more information is needed, ChoiceMarks help identify what kinds of questions to ask. When people are not clear about their objectives or information needs, ChoiceMarks can be used to help bring clarity to conversations. When decision making is stalled, ChoiceMarks can be used to uncover why.

ChoiceMarks acknowledge that decisions are made up of both logical and emotional elements. Decisions are made based on reason, research, and results. We also make decisions based on how we feel and what we have experienced. ChoiceMarks are the language and grammatical tools needed to end indecision, stop waffling, and start getting enough information to make a decision. The Power of No Model, described in my book *NO! How One Simple Word Can Transform Your Life* (AMACOM, 2005), is a series of questions designed to help us make a *yes* or *no* decision. Similarly, when stuck waffling with *maybes,* confusion, lack of team unity, or with no decisions being made, you can use ChoiceMarks to move a conversation or a group out of "stuck" and on to a decision.

Now that you know when the marks can best be used, let's define what the marks are. In brief, here are the five ChoiceMarks.

The Anti-Survival Mark

Picture a question mark upside down in a stop sign. Someone in anti-survival mode can be heard saying such things as, "I'm against this idea or approach because it is a bad idea or will cause me (us, the company) harm." In other words, the question is, "How can you prove to me that nothing will go wrong and *no* one will get hurt?" In statement form, the sentiment is, "If you can prove to me that nothing will go wrong and *no* one will get hurt, then I might agree to move to neutral or even to engaged enthusiasm to support the idea."

The anti-survival mark position means your instinct is telling you to stop, consider the situation, and determine whether to stay stopped or see that it is safe to move ahead. It tells a group that if everyone doesn't come to a full and complete stop to assess the situation, it's like running a stop sign and taking the risk of getting broadsided by oncoming traffic. The anti-survival mark may or may not result in a *no*. However, more often than not, it does result in a *no*—a nonnegotiable no that says this stops right here.

The Boxed-in Mark

Picture a question mark upside down in a square. Someone feeling boxed in can be heard saying, "I can't see how this would work," or, "We're not allowed to do this." The real question is, "How could this work?" And the statement is, "Show me how this could work, because if I can't see how it could work, I'll stay here, boxed in, quoting limitations and constraints, or I may even move to anti-survival and work against your idea." The boxed-in mark may, or may not, result in a *no*. The boxed-in mark position means that you are likely to stand in the way of a project moving forward.

The Neutral Mark

Picture a question mark in a caution circle. Someone feeling neutral might say, "I need more information before I'll make a decision," or, "I'm not going to stand in your way, but I'm not going to help you either." Internally, the person might be thinking, "I can ask questions because I'm not feeling emotionally attached to the final decision." In this case, the real question is, "Can I ask the questions I need answered?" or, "Can you move ahead and do this without me?" And the statements are, "Unless you let me ask for the information I need, I'll stay here waffling in neutral or I'll move toward anti-survival and work against the plan or idea." Another neutral statement is "I won't help you and I won't stand in your way, so just do it." The neutral mark may, or may not, result in a *no*. The neutral mark position means that you are not planning to stand in the way of the project and that you may or may not participate in getting the project done.

The Engaged Enthusiasm Mark

Now, picture a question mark in an exclamation mark. At this stage, someone is feeling excited about an idea and is ready to move forward to take action that will bring an idea or decision into existence. Phrases like, "I'm excited about this; let's get going," can be heard at this stage. An engaged enthusiasm mark person's question is, "What details do we need before we take action?" The statement is, "I'm ready to start, so let's pin down the details and make the project work." The engaged enthusiasm mark may, or may not, result in a *yes*. However, most often, it does result in a *yes*. The engaged enthusiasm mark position means that you are interested in the project and are willing to participate to see the project's completion.

The Extreme Excitement Mark

Because of the level of excitement, now picture an exclamation mark in a heart-shaped exclamation mark. Survival, high-intensity feeling, and positive action are the focus here, so you'll hear things like, "Isn't this exciting? Why aren't you on-board with us? Why do you want to hold us back?" These judgment-filled questions are really about the question, "What do you need to know to come along with this

idea and bring it into reality?" And the statement is, "I'm ready to move forward. You can come with us, or you can not participate; either way, we're moving forward. I'm committed to this and passionate about it. And I plan to move forward." The extreme excitement mark may or may not result in a *no* and most often results in a *yes*. The extreme excitement mark position means that your heart is in the project, your commitment is high, and you plan to participate.

Did you recognize yourself as a user of these ChoiceMarks (now that you have more detail than in Chapter 2)? Did you recognize people you work with? Did you recognize people you live with? Have you survived a team that couldn't make a decision because each team member was at a different stage in the Choice-Mark continuum?

All of the Marks are useful, valid, and important decision-making tools. Individually or as a group, an Anti-Survival Mark decision means we've determined that the potential harm outweighs any potential good and that we won't pursue the action. A boxed-in mark means one or more members of a team still has enough questions that could doom the project if not answered. A neutral mark means we can take action but that we might not be as successful as we could be if we'd answer more questions. An engaged enthusiasm mark means that most of the people in the discussion are excited about moving forward, clarifying the details for success, saying *yes*, and getting the task completed. And the use of an extreme excitement mark means that we're ready to move forward, with the majority of people fully supporting the decision and the actions that are to come next.

Getting Out of the Five Boxes: Moving from ChoiceMark to ChoiceMark

The next time you are stuck, stalled, or waffling on a decision, identify which ChoiceMark represents where you are. Then you can begin asking questions in order to make a decision, or at least identify the new ChoiceMark location that you've reached. Whenever a group is stalled or waffling, the same thing can be done.

Identify in which ChoiceMark location individual group members say they are. Then, stay in conversation and provide the needed information. Here are some tips to help move from one ChoiceMark to another so that a decision can be made.

Anti-Survival Marks

Remember, an anti-survival mark means that someone is feeling threatened or believes that the completion of the project is not worthwhile—and might even be unhealthy or dangerous to complete. In other words, fear, doubt, and disbelief are the foundation of anti-survival marks. People in anti-survival are signaling that they sense danger. Listen. They may be right. Listen for their questions and see what information you can share that will allow the person to move at least to neutral. To move out of anti-survival and into a new decision, these are some of the questions to ask:

1. What needs to change so that this decision becomes a safe decision?

2. What information do we need to move toward a neutral or excited position?

3. Whom do we need to involve to move out of anti-survival?

4. What will keep you in anti-survival?

5. What are you seeing, that we are failing to see, about the safety of doing this?

Anti-Survival is a good position to stay in when real danger is involved and making a *no* decision serves you or a group as a form of protection. Every opportunity is not always a good, ethical, or safe opportunity. In these cases, an anti-survival mark or decision is a good option.

Boxed-in Marks

Boxed-in marks show that doubt, disbelief, and, potentially, fear exist about the possibility of being able to accomplish what is being asked. To move out of boxed-in and into decision, these are some of the questions to ask:

1. What needs to change so that a *yes* decision becomes possible?

2. What information do we need to move toward a neutral or excited position?

3. What information would move us to anti-survival?

4. Who do we need to involve to move out of being boxed-in?

Boxed-in is a good position to stay in when reasonable options for completing the request have not been presented. It is also a good position to stay in when potential dangers have not been addressed or overcome. A boxed-in outlook can be used as a safety mechanism for helping the group make the most informed choices possible. Overuse of the boxed-in outlook can frustrate a group and prevent creative and best-possible decisions from being made.

Neutral Marks

Neutral marks show that neither doubt nor excitement is top-of-mind. A neutral mark reminds us that, "I may or may not participate." To move out of neutral and into a decision, these are some of the questions to ask:

1. What needs to change so that we will commit to a decision?

2. What information do we need to move toward an anti-survival or an excited position?

3. Whom do we need to involve to move ourselves out of neutral?

4. If you stay in neutral and we move forward, will you stand in our way? If you will stand in our way, what needs to change so that you won't?

Being in neutral is good when more questions still need to be explored to help a group make the best possible decision. If you choose to stay in neutral, it means that the group can move forward without your involvement and without your undermining the group's efforts.

Engaged Enthusiasm Marks

Engaged enthusiasm marks show that excitement exists for the completion of a request. People at the engaged enthusiasm mark stage have so much faith, hope, and excitement that they usually want others to be there with them. To move out of engaged enthusiasm and excitement and on into action, ask these questions:

1. Why do we need everyone to be at engaged enthusiasm or extreme excitement? In other words, do we really need to move others from where they are? (As long as no one blocks you, you can move forward with a decision.)

2. What questions still need to be answered to ensure our success?

3. When is the final deadline?

4. What is the budget?

5. Who is available to help?

6. Where will we find the resources and tools we need?

7. How will we be supported during the project?

8. Who are the best people to help achieve the goal? And how will we involve them on the project?

Engaged enthusiasm marks are good when genuine excitement in favor of a position, project, or action exists. Engaged enthusiasm marks can indicate that it is time to take action. However, engaged enthusiasm marks that don't include a review of and agreements on critical questions such as the above can be undermined by boxed-in mark thinking from people who weren't brought on-board, or at least brought to neutral before you moved forward with the project.

Extreme Excitement Marks

Extreme excitement marks show an abundance of energy, excitement, and willingness to move forward with passion to get the request or project completed. People at the extreme excitement mark stage have so much faith, hope, and excitement that they passionately want others to be here with them—and often expect others to be there with them. To move out of extreme excitement and into action, ask questions like these:

1. What would have to change to move us out of extreme excitement?

2. What needs to change so that this decision becomes one that everyone will participate in completing?

3. What information do we need to stay in the extreme excitement or excitement position?

4. Who do we need to involve to keep us at the extreme excitement level?

5. What's holding us back from making this decision right now?

Extreme excitement marks are good when there is genuine passion and excitement and a willingness to participate in getting a project, task, or request completed. If you are not willing to participate, you are at the neutral or engaged enthusiasm mark position, rather than the extreme excitement mark position. Remember, the engaged enthusiasm mark position means your heart is in the project, your commitment is high, and you plan to participate. Like engaged enthusiasm marks, extreme excitement marks can undermine a project's success when people with boxed-in mark thinking aren't brought on-board, or at least brought to neutral before you move forward with the project.

In order to gain some skill in recognizing the five ChoiceMarks, the practices that follow provide an opportunity to both identify and implement ChoiceMark decision points and language for moving to a final decision.

Moving Out of a Box: ChoiceMarks Practice— ChoiceMarks at Work

No doubt, you've been in a position similar to the following:

A team meeting is breaking down. Two people are standing and working their way to the door to leave. Four other people are in deep and emotional conversation about what needs to be done next. And three others are sitting at the table, not even appearing to listen to the conversation. The scheduled end of the meeting is still thirty minutes away. A decision is needed today, or you'll miss out on a customer opportunity that would bring in a six-figure sale with a new client.

Questions to Ask Once You Have ChoiceMarks as Decision Tools

Now that you have ChoiceMarks as decision tools, what can you do to help save this meeting and get a decision to be made? Ask the following:

1. How many people are potentially in anti-survival mode?

2. How many people are in boxed-in, engaged enthusiasm, or extreme excitement?

3. How many people are in neutral?

4. What questions will you ask to get those with anti-survival marks to participate in the discussion and decision making?

5. What questions will you ask to determine who is boxed-in and who is at engaged enthusiasm?

6. What questions will you ask to get those in neutral to participate in the discussion and decision making?

7. What will you and the group accept as the minimum involvement before moving on with a positive decision to take to this new client?

8. What information from a boxed-in or anti-survival mark person would keep you from taking on this new client?

Possible Answers

1. How many people are potentially in anti-survival mode? Two to five. The people by the door and the people at the table could be in anti-survival.

2. How many people are in boxed-in, engaged enthusiasm, or extreme excitement? Four—the people at the table in conversation.

3. How many people are in neutral? Perhaps three—the people at the table looking like they are somewhere else. But they could be in anti-survival or boxed in.

4. What questions will you ask to get those with anti-survival marks to participate in the discussion and decision making? "What will keep us from doing this successfully?" or, "What's been your experience? We haven't had a chance to hear from you."

5. What questions will you ask to determine who is boxed-in and who is at engaged enthusiasm? "What aren't we considering that we should be?" or, "What emotions are blinding us to the possibilities?"

6. What questions will you ask to get those in neutral to participate in the discussion and decision making? "What information do we need to share to bring everyone into an active role on this project?" or, "What questions haven't been asked yet?"

7. What will you and the group accept as the minimum involvement before moving on with a positive decision to take on this new client? You may need everyone's expertise and therefore everyone's participation. Or, you may be able to move forward with a few people, freeing those who are interested in helping on this project to stay focused on the areas they are already working on. Or, you may think you can move forward without leaving anyone feeling left out, only to discover a few months later that someone is unhappy, or so unhappy that the project is being undermined.

8. What information from a boxed-in or anti-survival mark person would keep you from taking on this new client? Discovery that the client doesn't pay, that the project has risks you weren't aware of, or discovery that other vendors have already suffered from trying to deliver what the client wants.

Moving Out of a Box: ChoiceMark Practice— ChoiceMarks in Our Personal Decision Making

Now let's visit Jane's very personal story from a well-remembered birthday celebration. Jane is a colleague of Jana's who shared this decision-making story from her young adulthood. Jane's message is that learning to make good decisions is a lifetime journey and that knowing what she knows now about making decisions, she could have made better decisions during this birthday celebration. Making ever-better and best-possible decisions is truly a lifetime's work of skill building. Here's the story, in Jane's words. As you read the story in full, you'll discover that at certain times in the story, nearly every sentence is a decision point.

It was my 30th birthday. My girlfriend and I headed up to Garland, Michigan, to celebrate my December birthday. We went one week before the huge holiday rush at the lodge. It was a Thursday night and the five-star restaurant was empty except for us. I felt as though we were in the movie *The Shining*. The waitress was wonderful and gave us great service and a free after-dinner drink in the lounge.

Snow had been falling all night and the snow-removal crew had just come into the lounge after plowing. The waitress was just closing and gave them their last drink. She asked if we wanted to join them all at their favorite pub. My girlfriend immediately committed. I was not surprised, but went along with the plans, thinking she would drive so that we could always leave early. The next thing I knew, on the way out to the car, the waitress and two of the guys volunteered to drive us in their Jeep. I found myself saying *no* in my heart, while my head was shaking *yes*. The waitress, whom I'd known for 90 minutes, seemed credible. I expressed my uneasiness to my girlfriend and she convinced me that everything would be fine. We drove and drove. It seemed like forever. We ended up at a local deer hunter's bar where we met the rest of our group. Needless to say they were all dressed in appropriate "up north" cold-weather wear, while we were dressed up and decked to the nines, including high-heel shoes.

I was starting to feel trapped, yet once again, I went against my intuition and continued to go with the crowd. We played pool, had a few beers, and listened to numerous songs by Bob Seger. People were dancing, talking, and drinking until the bar closed. Our "wonderful" waitress was *no* where to be seen—she had left with her boyfriend. So, our only way back to the lodge was with the twenty-something year olds in their Jeep. I thought *no*. I told them I would just call a cab. They all laughed because the nearest taxi was over 45 miles away and only provided service during the day. Reluctantly, I got in the backseat of the Jeep and threatened my girlfriend if she didn't get in the back with me. I knew I should have said stop and *no* to this grand adventure when the owner of the Jeep refused to give his friend the keys to drive. His friend kept insisting, saying he wasn't going to go with him, but once again, we all ended up compromising and letting him drive.

As we turned out of the bar and headed down the snow covered road at 50 miles per hour, I realized we were going away from the lodge where our car was parked. I pleaded for the driver to stop and let us get out. He just laughed and spun down a fire lane. I hit my head on the roll-bar and my knees. He kept driving in four-wheel drive and we were on our way down the fire lane with at least a foot of snow.

The next thing I know, he exclaimed, "I hope this is frozen, or we are all going swimming." I was screaming, "Let me out!" At this time, my girlfriend was holding on for dear life, and the guy in the passenger seat was starting to tell his friend, "This is not funny anymore." He pleaded for five minutes, which seemed like hours, to get him to turn around, get off the lake, and get back on land. We were about two hundred yards out on one of the spring-fed lakes, with *no* houses anywhere to be seen. Finally, after realizing *no* one was joining him in his fun, he barreled back down the fire trail, came back out onto a highway, and spun around 180 degrees just in time to miss a vehicle heading down our lane.

I had started saying prayers at the very minute we started home, asking "please get us home safely in whatever way possible." The next thing I knew, the car that had almost hit us turned abruptly around with red and white lights came on. I don't think I was ever so glad to be pulled over by the County Sheriff's department. After several humiliating questions in the back of the police car, we were advised we would need to get back in the Jeep to get a ride back to the lodge. The police knew the driver and his friend, so only gave them a warning and let them go. I refused to get out of the back of the police car. The policemen said they could not drive us back to the lodge. I said, "No, I am not going to get in that Jeep, and will you call a cab for us." The police finally laughed to see just how gullible we were, and took us back to the lodge with all of their lights on and all of the maintenance and hotel staff gathering to see what the commotion was about.

Needless to say, the next morning we did not go down to the restaurant for breakfast, we ordered room service. It was delivered by our friend, the crazy driver, and I refused to open the door to the room. We called the desk and had our bill sent to our home and we quickly exited. I was more educated about the importance of listening to my gut when it comes to verbalizing what my heart and my gut are telling me.

ChoiceMark Practice Directions

For each of the 18 decision points that are listed below, identify which Choice-Mark Jane could have used or did use to ask for more information. Circle the ChoiceMarks that identify each decision point. Then write a question that she could have asked.

1. "I felt as though we were in the movie *The Shining.* The waitress was wonderful and gave us great service and a free after-dinner drink in the lounge."
Anti-Survival
Boxed-in
Neutral
Engaged Enthusiasm
Extreme Excitement
Question you would have asked: _____

2. "The waitress was just closing and gave them their last drink. She asked if we wanted to join them all at their favorite pub."
Anti-Survival
Boxed-in
Neutral
Engaged Enthusiasm
Extreme Excitement
Question you would have asked: _____

3. "My girlfriend immediately committed."
Anti-Survival
Boxed-in

Neutral
Engaged Enthusiasm
Extreme Excitement
Question you would have asked: _____

4. "I was not surprised, but went along with the plans, thinking she would drive so that we could always leave early."
Anti-Survival
Boxed-in
Neutral
Engaged Enthusiasm
Extreme Excitement
Question you would have asked: _____

5. "The next thing I knew, on the way out to the car, the waitress and two of the guys volunteered to drive us in their Jeep."
Anti-Survival
Boxed-in
Neutral
Engaged Enthusiasm
Extreme Excitement
Question you would have asked: _____

6. "I found myself saying no in my heart, while my head was shaking yes."
Anti-Survival
Boxed-in
Neutral
Engaged Enthusiasm
Extreme Excitement
Question you would have asked: _____

7. "I expressed my uneasiness to my girlfriend and she convinced me that everything would be fine."
Anti-Survival
Boxed-in
Neutral
Engaged Enthusiasm
Extreme Excitement
Question you would have asked: _____

8. "They were all dressed in appropriate 'up north' cold-weather wear and we were dressed up and decked to the nines, including high-heel shoes."
Anti-Survival
Boxed-in

Neutral
Engaged Enthusiasm
Extreme Excitement
Question you would have asked: _____

9. "I was starting to feel trapped, yet once again, I went against my intuition and continued to go with the crowd."
Anti-Survival
Boxed-in
Neutral
Engaged Enthusiasm
Extreme Excitement
Question you would have asked: _____

10. "Our 'wonderful' waitress was *no* where to be seen—she had left with her boyfriend. So, our only way back to the lodge was with the twenty-something year olds in their Jeep. I thought *no*. I told them I would just call a cab."
Anti-Survival
Boxed-in
Neutral
Engaged Enthusiasm
Extreme Excitement
Question you would have asked: _____

11. "They all laughed because the nearest taxi was over 45 miles away and only provided service during the day."
Anti-Survival
Boxed-in
Neutral
Engaged Enthusiasm
Extreme Excitement
Question you would have asked: _____

12. "I knew I should have said *stop* and *no* to this grand adventure when the owner of the Jeep refused to give his friend the keys to drive."
Anti-Survival
Boxed-in
Neutral
Engaged Enthusiasm
Extreme Excitement
Question you would have asked: _____

13. "His friend kept insisting, saying he wasn't going to go with him, but once again, we all ended up compromising and letting him drive."

Anti-Survival
Boxed-in
Neutral
Engaged Enthusiasm
Extreme Excitement
Question you would have asked: _____

14. "As we turned out of the bar and headed down the snow covered road at 50 miles per hour, I realized we were going away from the lodge where our car was parked. I pleaded for the driver to stop and let us get out."
Anti-Survival
Boxed-in
Neutral
Engaged Enthusiasm
Extreme Excitement
Question you would have asked: _____

15. "He just laughed and spun down a fire lane. I hit my head on the roll-bar and my knees. He kept driving in four-wheel drive and we were on our way down the fire lane with at least a foot of snow."
Anti-Survival
Boxed-in
Neutral
Engaged Enthusiasm
Extreme Excitement
Question you would have asked: _____

16. "The next thing I know, he exclaimed, 'I hope this is frozen, or we are all going swimming.' I was screaming 'Let me out!' At this time, my girlfriend was holding on for dear life, and the guy in the passenger seat was starting to tell his friend, 'This is not funny anymore.'"
Anti-Survival
Boxed-in
Neutral
Engaged Enthusiasm
Extreme Excitement
Question you would have asked: _____

17. "I refused to get out of the back of the police car. The policemen said they could not drive us back to the lodge. I said, 'No, I am not going to get in that Jeep, and will you call a cab for us.'"
Anti-Survival
Boxed-in
Neutral

Engaged Enthusiasm
Extreme Excitement
Question you would have asked: _____

18. "The next morning we did not go down to the restaurant for breakfast, we ordered room service. It was delivered by our friend, the crazy driver, and I refused to open the door to the room. We called the desk and had our bill sent to our home and we quickly exited."
Anti-Survival
Boxed-in
Neutral
Engaged Enthusiasm
Extreme Excitement
Question you would have asked: _____

Possible Answers

The best-answer ChoiceMarks are listed for each of the 18 decision points. A potential question that she could have asked is also listed.

1. "I felt as though we were in the movie *The Shining*. The waitress was wonderful and gave us great service and a free after-dinner drink in the lounge."
   Boxed-in at first, then neutral in the second sentence.
   Questions that could have been asked: Where is everybody tonight? With the holidays, when do you close tonight?

2. "The waitress was just closing and gave them their last drink. She asked if we wanted to join them all at their favorite pub."
   Engaged enthusiasm.
   Questions that could have been asked: Where is the pub? How far away is it?

3. "My girlfriend immediately committed."
   Extreme excitement drove the girlfriend's decision, although it may not have been the best-possible place to respond from.
   Questions that could have been asked: How far away is it? How late will you be staying?

4. "I was not surprised, but went along with the plans, thinking she would drive so that we could always leave early."
   Boxed-in.
   Questions that could have been asked: Can we follow you in our car?

5. "The next thing I knew, on the way out to the car, the waitress and two of the guys volunteered to drive us in their Jeep."

Boxed-in.

Questions that could have been asked: What are the directions to this place? Can we follow you in our car?

6. "I found myself saying no in my heart, while my head was shaking yes."

Anti-survival.

Questions that could have been asked: Are we really sure about this? Couldn't we do something else next? What else can we do tonight, that feels more safe?

7. "I expressed my uneasiness to my girlfriend and she convinced me that everything would be fine."

Anti-survival and boxed-in.

Questions that could have been asked: How do you know everything will be fine?

8. "They were all dressed in appropriate 'up north' cold-weather wear and we were dressed up and decked to the nines, including high-heel shoes."

Anti-survival because of the mismatch of attire. It was winter in Michigan.

Questions that could have been asked: What are we doing here—we aren't even dressed for this?

9. "I was starting to feel trapped, yet once again, I went against my intuition and continued to go with the crowd."

Anti-survival.

Questions that could have been asked: Why am I feeling so uneasy? What do I need to do about this?

10. "Our 'wonderful' waitress was *no* where to be seen—she had left with her boyfriend. So, our only way back to the lodge was with the twenty-something year olds in their Jeep. I thought *no*. I told them I would just call a cab."

Boxed-in and some anti-survival.

Questions that could have been asked: Who will call a cab? What other options are there?

11. "They all laughed because the nearest taxi was over 45 miles away and only provided service during the day."

Anti-survival: feeling like no options were available.

Questions that could have been asked: What other options are there? Who else could take us back?

12. "I knew I should have said *stop* and *no* to this grand adventure when the owner of the Jeep refused to give his friend the keys to drive."

Anti-survival.

Questions that could have been asked: What other options are there? Why don't you let me drive?

13. "His friend kept insisting, saying he wasn't going to go with him, but once again, we all ended up compromising and letting him drive."
Anti-survival and boxed-in.
Questions that could have been asked: Who else can drive the Jeep back?

14. "As we turned out of the bar and headed down the snow covered road at 50 miles per hour, I realized we were going away from the lodge where our car was parked. I pleaded for the driver to stop and let us get out."
Anti-survival and extreme excitement. Jane's anti-survival questions had been running wild, so out of fear, her extreme excitement kicked in and she wanted out of the car.
Questions that could have been asked: Aren't we headed away from the lodge? Will you please take us right back to the lodge?

15. "He just laughed and spun down a fire lane. I hit my head on the roll-bar and my knees. He kept driving in four-wheel drive and we were on our way down the fire lane with at least a foot of snow."
Anti-survival.
Questions that could have been asked of the friend: Where are we going? Why don't you do something?

16. "The next thing I know, he exclaimed, 'I hope this is frozen, or we are all going swimming.' I was screaming 'Let me out!' At this time, my girlfriend was holding on for dear life and the guy in the passenger seat was starting to tell his friend, 'This is not funny anymore.'"
Anti-survival.
Questions that could have been asked: Why don't you stop and let us out?

17. "I refused to get out of the back of the police car. The policemen said they could not drive us back to the lodge. I said, 'No, I am not going to get in that Jeep, and will you call a cab for us.'"
Anti-survival and extreme excitement. Again, Jane's anti-survival instincts were in full force, her extreme excitement kicked in and she refused to get out of the police car.
Questions that could have been asked: Why can't you take us back? Who else will you find to take us back? Why are you putting us at risk again?

18. "The next morning we did not go down to the restaurant for breakfast, we ordered room service. It was delivered by our friend, the crazy driver, and I refused to open the door to the room. We called the desk and had our bill sent to our home and we quickly exited."

Boxed-in. They couldn't get away from the crazy driver.

Questions that could have been asked at the end of the experience: What did we learn from our experience?

What Does It All Mean?

Why is it important to look for decision points so carefully? Because, by listening for data, comments, and stories that point to ChoiceMark locations along a decision-making continuum, individuals and groups can move to make a decision and eliminate the need to make even more decisions later. Just like every line in a computer program commands an action to be taken, sometimes every sentence someone speaks is giving us information about how, why, and when that person will make a decision. And when a group wants to move forward with a clear sense of the work to be done —or not to be done—recognizing the ChoiceMarks being used lets the group members identify whether anyone will block the work that at least part of the team wants to take forward. Recognizing which ChoiceMarks are being addressed during someone's comments or presentations can help you as a group leader and as a team participant to move the team to make a decision. In other words, better and more actionable decisions will result from each discussion in which you apply the ChoiceMarks.

Chapter Summary

ChoiceMarks as decision tools can help individuals and groups make better decisions. The ChoiceMarks are

Anti-Survival,

Boxed-in,

Neutral,

Engaged Enthusiasm, and

Extreme Excitement.

When stuck in one of the marks, conversation and question asking can help move individuals and teams out of one box and on to a ChoiceMark continuum location that allows a decision to be made and appropriate follow-up action to be taken.

Actively listen for the decision points being presented in a conversation. Then determine which ChoiceMark best depicts the speaker's point of view. Next, start asking questions (which you'll find many more of in the chapters ahead and in the appendix) in order to learn more about the person's point of view and so that you can provide information that allows for decision making.

CHAPTER 4

Managing Extreme Excitement

"Extreme" Is In

Over the last two decades, the phrase "extreme sports" has become part of cultures around the world. Extreme sporting activities range from snowboarding and helicopter skiing to storm chasing and bungee jumping. These extreme sports have the common elements of speed; adventure; physical demands that many people choose not to pursue; an adrenaline rush; and even the experience of outright danger. Another common element of extreme sports is that they tend to be individual pursuits rather than team sports. People pursuing extreme sports are passionate about what they do and where they go. Often spending time to research locations and money to get there, extreme sports enthusiasts are committed to heightening their adventures. Today, people of all ages pursue extreme sports.

The relevance of an extreme sports discussion to decision making is multiple-fold. First, recognize that the individual nature of extreme sports could lead to the conclusion that decision making is an individual undertaking which is more likely to be true of command-and-control style decision makers than consensus-oriented decision makers. The command-and-control approach to decision making corresponds to the extreme excitement consensus stage. Here's how. When a person or a team is at extreme excitement but unfamiliar with the ChoiceMarks and therefore less able to articulate why they are at this decision stage, their forge-ahead-with-immediacy attitude can come across as command-and-control decision direction. People in any kind of extreme excitement typically forget to listen to the details of what others are communicating because the focus on the task (or adventure) at hand is so great. And in the heightened excitement, a limited listening ability contributes to the appearance of being in command-and-control mode.

Next, like extreme sports, the extreme excitement stage of consensus building demands high levels of energy. The high-energy demand is relevant because the extreme excitement stage brings with it an energy level that can affect others' willingness to participate in decision making and in implementation. If the extreme excitement is too high, others may opt out of participating in the decision and in implementation. If the extreme excitement includes an ongoing ability to listen and respond to others' concerns, successful implementation is more likely. The extreme excitement stage also demands a lot of energy when a meeting leader or a meeting participant tries to get others to join the decision agreement at the extreme excitement stage. Recall from Chapter 1 that everyone brings their own experiences and mindsets to each decision discussion. Given our different life experiences it is unlikely that entire teams will reach the same level of enthusiasm or excitement for every decision.

Third, the level of passion in the pursuit of each extreme sport is so high that nothing stands in the way of pursuing the adventure. And in a similar way, people at the extreme excitement stage of reaching consensus see no reason for anything to stand in their way of getting things done. High passion and commitment to action characterize the extreme excitement stage. In fact, the passion and commitment to act can be so overwhelming that they can also cause others to believe a person is acting in a command-and-control manner and not taking into account as many ideas as consensus-driven decisions request.

Interestingly, extreme excitement is often the place that teams and group leaders head when focused on reaching a decision. This mistakenly comes from the belief that extreme excitement must be achieved in order to truly have reached consensus. Extreme excitement is heightened support for a "yes" or "let's do it" decision. Reaching extreme excitement with an entire group when focused on reaching consensus is a rare occurrence. Day-to-day decision-making reality is that extreme excitement may happen on the part of a few individuals, one individual, or none of the individuals in the decision-making body. The day-to-day reality also is that so rarely will an entire decision-making group reach the level of extreme excitement that our business, cultural, and societal stories and even myths don't include recognizable and repeatable examples.

Why talk about extreme excitement as one of the five stages of reaching consensus? For two reasons: first, because there are individuals who reach extreme excitement when decision making and second, because believing that everyone must reach extreme excitement in order to achieve consensus is wrong and unproductive.

When Individuals Reach Extreme Excitement

Individuals reach extreme excitement for a variety of reasons. Personal interest, study, or experience may ignite someone's passion. A family tragedy, unexpected death, or horrible treatment may feed someone's passion. Extraordinary commitment to problem solving or research may fuel someone's passion. Whatever its cause, extreme excitement is characterized by passion, high energy, a near unwillingness to listen to other points of view (which you'll read more about in anti-survival, too), and an above-usual enthusiasm for seeing something happen.

When individuals reach extreme excitement there are times that redirecting or expanding their focus can be difficult because of the already high level of commitment to take action. In order to get other ideas and input heard by people already in extreme excitement, present information in ways that will validate the excitement and at the same time offer opposing points of view, describe potential challenges or barriers, and invite an enlarged consideration of what action is best to agree to move forward upon. When presenting information that challenges the positions of people in extreme excitement, be prepared for push-back, upset, and even anger. Stay your course and continue to state your information, concerns, and case because decision making does not require everyone to be in extreme excitement for a decision to be made.

Groups Don't Need to Reach Extreme Excitement to Make Decisions

While individuals who have reached extreme excitement believe that others should join them, the reality is that most people have limited or even no workplace topics or items that move them to extreme excitement. As a result, it is time for groups to stop believing that getting everyone to extreme excitement is the goal of consensus. Instead, consider that any time a group can make a decision with no one blocking it or its implementation as a decision victory and move on. What this means is that as long as no one person, or no subset group plans to prevent or stand in the way of a decision and its implementation, then the group can make a decision and move forward.

Over the years, I've served on a number of nonprofit boards. These board groups are frequently decision-making bodies that include one or more individuals whose passion runs high for the cause and leans them toward extreme excitement consensus building. I recall one board meeting where a new fund raising event was being discussed with great enthusiasm. Not having joined the board on account of my fund raising expertise, I was neutral about the whole thing and had not spoken up in favor or against the event idea. Suddenly several heads turned my way as the extremely excited board chair swiveled my direction while asking, "Jana, what do you think? Isn't this great, really great?" From my neutral position, I calmly said, "Fund raising is not my area of expertise or interest. I really don't have any input." He then said, "Well, can't we get you excited about this and about helping out by being in the dunk booth?"

"No," I said, "however, I'm not standing in your way. You can go ahead without me. Really." Then, several other board members cajoled me and I again said, "Really, it's okay. I'm sure it will be fun but I'm not working on this event." Finally, still in extreme excitement, the other board members went ahead without me. The event went well and raised about the amount that was desired.

This experience points out the need for individuals who are already committed to a decision at the extreme excitement stage to really listen to what else is being said by team members. And to attentively discern whether anyone is actually standing in the way or suggesting that a "don't do it" decision be made. If no one stands in the way of moving forward, a go-ahead decision can still be made. However, when an individual or a team moves into extreme excitement, the momentum for "do it" or "decide in favor of this" can become so great that real and legitimate concerns don't get heard. There is danger in not hearing about concerns or pitfalls because such things as staff availability, realistic budgets, and safety can end up being overlooked when excitement runs high. Best-possible decision making takes into account relevant information that is both in favor of a decision and is opposed to a decision. In other words, best-possible decision making is dependent on a decision discussion that leads to the final decision. At all five ChoiceMarks, stages of consensus, discussion, question asking, and listening skills are needed.

Decision-Making Discussion Tips

Here are some communication tips that will improve the effectiveness and success of each decision-making opportunity.

a. Share your own point of view when asked to, or when appropriate to do so. One of the challenges of consensus-driven decision making is hearing from people who have relevant ideas and viewpoints to share. So, when you have something to contribute be sure to speak up during the discussion.

b. Share your own experience and knowledge. You are on the team because you have relevant experience, expertise, and knowledge. Again, speak up and share what you know about how things can work or how things might go.

c. Listen to other people's points of view to learn how your own point of view can expand or change. Another challenge during information-gathering discussions is that individual viewpoints can prevail to the point of prematurely narrowing the discussion. Listen for opinions and insights that can improve the decision to be made and the implementation plan to be built.

d. Listen to other people's experience and knowledge. Everyone on the team has or should have relevant experience and knowledge to share. Hear them out. Listen for pros, cons, and useful details.

e. Recognize when enough information has been shared and when it is time to reach a decision. One of the complaints about consensus-driven decision making is, "All we ever do is talk. When will a decision get made?" Every discussion hits a turning point that becomes a decision point for talking more or moving on to agree upon and reach a decision.

f. Reach a decision. That's it. Decision-making discussions must reach a decision or all that is happening is talk. Today's workplaces have little time for talk that doesn't lead to action.

g. Commit to implementation of the decision and accepting personal tasks to accomplish. Once a decision has been made, help get it implemented. Or, stay out of the way of the team members who committed to implementation.

Question-Asking Tips

Effective question-asking skills include the following:

a. Use task-oriented questions. The agenda for a meeting or discussion outlines the tasks and topics to be addressed. Task-oriented questions focus on agenda items, topic details, specifics, measures and benchmarks, standards, quantitative and qualitative measures, time frames, deadlines, budgets, and resource details. Task-oriented questions include: "Where are we on the agenda? How much budget will we need? What is the deadline we have to meet?"

b. Use relationship-oriented questions. When the level of willingness to work together is unclear, it's time to ask relationship-oriented questions. For example, "What's standing in our way right now? Who else needs to be included before we reach a decision? How will our making this decision affect the departments we work with?" Another approach is to take a break: "Why don't we take a break and come back in ten minutes?" This allows a cooling-off time and an opportunity for some one-on-one conversations to uncover where the breakdowns in the conversation are occurring.

c. Use process-oriented questions. Coming to consensus is a process, as are command-and-control decision making, brainstorming, making motions, and voting. Most problem solving and project management systems include clear steps and discussion points. So, a process-oriented question is one that focuses on steps, sequences, and procedures or manners and methods for getting work accomplished and getting decisions made. Process-oriented questions sound like, "Have we generated enough ideas that we can move to making a decision now? We're not reaching consensus and we have to make a decision today, so can we take a vote to determine how to move forward?" And a process-oriented suggestion includes the making of a motion: "I move that we approve this new product idea for a market research study to be completed and for a production research team to tell us what it would take to make it. Both teams are to report back to this group by the 27th of this month."

d. Use tones and volumes of voice that invite people to speak up. When others can't even physically hear what you have to say they won't listen. When others can't hear your question because of hearing aids, hearing loss, room-noise distractions, or hallway noise distractions, they won't respond to your question.

e. Use open-ended questions for consensus oriented decision discussions. "What..." starts questions that lead to shared information, ideas, and expertise. "Who..." starts a question meant to reveal who can help, who is needed before the decision is made, and who will be affected by decisions. "Where..." starts a question in search of locations, data sources, and studies that can contribute to the discussion and decision. "When ..." starts a question looking to pin down deadlines, time frames, time requirements, and timing of action sequences. "Why..." can be the start of a defensive discussion. Most "why" questions can be rephrased into "what" questions. For example "Why did you do it that way?" can be rephrased into the question "What information or experience lead to the decision to do it this way?" And "Why did it break down?" can be rephrased into the question "What caused the breakdown?" Finally, the open-ended question starter "How." How starts a question that is in search of process suggestions, sequences, and steps for solving a problem or building an implementation plan. "How can we ensure the successful implementation of our decision?"

f. Use closed-ended questions when moving into command-and-control decision making: did, will, can, was, or is. Closed-ended questions result in "yes" or "no" responses. Open-ended questions are like essay questions looking for longer answers. Closed-ended questions are looking for the forced-choice answer of yes or no. Examples of closed-ended questions include, "Is enough of the budget still available? Do we have trained staff ready to handle this production change? Will our current systems handle the increase in production demand?" During discussions, closed-ended questions are sometimes followed up by open-ended questions. For instance, "Do we have trained staff ready to handle this production change?" elicits the answer "Yes" which is followed by the open-ended question "Who?"

g. Ask the question and be quiet. We've all seen the antithesis of this, the meeting leader who asks for input, poses a question, and then answers the question. This is not effective. When asking a question, ask it, and then listen. Keep listening even when responses seem slow to come forward. Some groups are more reflective than others and require ample processing time before speaking up. Keep quiet and listen even if the moments of silence seem painfully long.

Listening Tips

Effective listening skills include the following:

a. Listen for key words. Key words communicate the real message of the speaker. At church recently, a developmentally challenged woman behind us demonstrated that while her body prevented her active participation, her brain was capturing the pastor's key words. She was able to repeat the phrases as "be more, God's call, on purpose, and give time." Listen. We can all find the key words to focus in on a speaker's message.

b. Listen for tones and volume of voice. The louder someone is, the more likely they are communicating to the group that they don't feel heard. The quieter someone is speaking, the more likely they are hesitant about the value of what they are contributing. An angry tone of voice is just that, angry. So use an open-ended question to find out "What is it that you want us to hear?"

c. Watch for body language that signals concern, discomfort, or excitement. Acknowledge what you've observed by asking an open-ended statement and question sequence such as "I sense some stress in the room right now, what needs to be on the table?" or, "I see some excitement for this approach. What will allow us to move forward with it?"

d. Observe the spoken and unspoken levels of people's willingness to work together. This is relationship listening.

e. Employ task listening. Similar to task-oriented question asking, task listening focuses on details, data, specifics, timelines, budgets, measures, staffing levels, and safety concerns.

   f. Employ procedural listening. Similar to process-oriented question asking, procedural listening focuses on identifying steps, sequences, methods, processes, and checklist items.

   g. Acknowledge what others say. Acknowledgement can occur in a variety of forms: paraphrasing back what someone has said; recording a person's ideas in writing on a flipchart on in the minutes; or by inviting further comment by asking a question or saying, "That's an interesting approach, tell us more about it."

Whatever your current communication skills are, they can always be improved. If you've mastered the basics (items a through d in each of the above discussion, question-asking, and listening tips sections), then move on to master the nuances of the skills described in e, f, and g of the preceding three tips sections. Whether or not you've ever found yourself at the extreme excitement level of consensus, you may at some point in your professional or personal life come across a decision that moves you to extreme excitement.

Questions to Ask When You Are in Extreme Excitement

When you are the person in extreme excitement it is easy to be blindsided by obstacles and barriers that you overlooked. It is also easy for others to think you are being unreasonable in your high excitement. To prevent yourself from being marginalized or prevented from reaching the goal, ask others for their input. Consider asking any one of the following questions in order to expand your point of view and your understanding of what experiences others have that can lead you and the team to an even better decision and implementation plan.

- What are your thoughts?
- What are your ideas?
- What ideas should I also be taking into consideration?
- What experiences have you had with problems like this?
- What results have you seen in the past?
- How can I avoid any barriers that have happened in the past?
- What other approaches might work?
- Where could we visit to see the ideas in action?
- When is a realistic timetable for implementation?

- How many resources will we need?
- Where in our own organization is this already working?

Questions to Ask When Others Are in Extreme Excitement

A person in extreme excitement is convinced and convicted of their position. Rightly or wrongly this person is committed to a viewpoint and is generally hopeful that the rest of the group members will be excited and committed too. Acknowledge the excitement and engage in a conversation. Your questions and ideas may change the decision outcome. If the decision outcome is not changed by your input, at least the discussion has been enlarged enough to address potential pitfalls. You can seek more information from someone in extreme excitement by asking questions or making information invitations such as the following:

- Help me understand what leads you to this conclusion.
- How do you know that this is the best course of action?
- When do you see implementation occurring?
- What kind of budget will be needed to make this happen?
- What project plan will we need to make this work?
- When are the deadlines going to be?
- Where will the resources come from for implementation?
- Can you share your vision for the rollout?
- Can you outline the project timeline for us?
- Who has done this successfully already?
- Who can help get this done?

Just Because Someone Reaches Extreme Excitement, Don't Expect Something to Get Done

Extreme excitement can be a permanent state of being, making decisions and getting work done. It also can be a temporary state of commitment. Before a decision-making meeting ends, be sure to secure commitment for follow-up actions and decision implementation. Also before the end of every meeting, clearly state who is responsible for getting what done and by what deadline. Then, enthusiastically encourage the extreme excitement team member(s) to achieve the result and to let you know if any help or resources are needed along the way. Use phrases such as, "Thanks for taking this on with so much gusto (enthusiasm). Let us know what you want help with along the way."

Recall the hoopla surrounding the same-industry synergy of the Daimler-Benz and Chrysler Corporation merger of 1998. The extreme excitement about all of the great product improvements and sales growth that could come from the merger quickly faded to neutral, and by late 2007 DaimlerChrysler was split up into separate entities again. This is an example of how early excitement does not always lead to the intended results and can then lead to new decision demands. It also proves that decisions of all sizes demand a strong implementation plan to ensure success.

To ensure decision implementation, check in periodically on the progress toward the agreed-upon results. Extreme excitement stage people can sometimes get distracted from the original agreement on outcomes. They also can move ahead so forcefully that needed input is not gathered along the way. On the positive side, teams in extreme excitement that have gathered critical input along the way can achieve above-average results and creativity during implementation. You can additionally invite input between meeting implementation and follow-through by using phrases such as these: "Just checking in, how are things going? Any problems? Any challenges coming up that we need to address? Let me know if you need anything to get this done. Have you encountered any roadblocks? What can we do to overcome the roadblocks? How are things going? What successes are you having?" Remember to really pause and listen. When help is most needed is often the time when people are most reluctant to speak up.

With this information in hand, you are ready to practice recognizing ChoiceMark decision points and selecting language that you can use to move decision discussions forward to an actual decision. In this chapter and the ChoiceMark focused Chapters 5, 6, 7, and 8, you'll have four scenarios in which to practice identifying discussion decision points and crafting language that would work in the scenario to move the team toward a decision. These practices are designed for you to build your skills and confidence as a decision maker, as a team leader, and as a team member.

ChoiceMark Practices

Read through each scenario. Watch for decision point language and signals. Respond to the questions at the end of each scenario. Also identify which of the four scenarios are similar to situations you've experienced. Then consider how you can now go back and handle your own decision situations with greater effectiveness.

Scenario 1—Recognizing Extreme Excitement in Action

Sometimes extreme excitement is loud and visible. Other times it is subtle. In this purchasing department staff meeting, identify the two people who are demonstrating extreme excitement.

Every Thursday morning, the Alpharet Company purchasing department holds a staff meeting for the purpose of identifying new products needed by the company, updating request for proposal (RFP), and updating back-ordered products that may require finding new suppliers. Cedric Fredricksen is the meeting leader and is also the director for the purchasing department. The attendees at the meeting include Joe Anderson, purchasing specialist; Janet Hernandez, purchasing specialist; Fred Alverez, RFP issuing agent; and Vic Toney, vendor relations specialist. Absent from the meeting is Cynthia Thorngaard, who is the quality control specialist. The staff meeting has already begun and discussion has stalled during the decision making stage of prioritizing new products to purchase. Thirty minutes into a one-hour meeting no decisions have been reached and there are still six items remaining on the agenda that need attention. Nearly everyone is frustrated.

Cedric: Okay. We have talked about six potential products and we only need two. One has to fill the production department's request for machine oil. And the other decision we need to make is on the request for new meeting room light bulbs. I appreciate all of the input you have each given.

Janet: I think we have enough information to go with MeetingElectrics for the light bulbs. And they have a good track record.

Vic: I agree with Janet. And, I've met with MeetingElectrics' president several times in the last six months. They really want our business and I think they'll work hard to meet our needs and keep our business. Let's approve an initial order with them.

Fred: Wait, we haven't even issued a RFP for this product. How can we approve purchasing new products without input from Cynthia about meeting our quality specifications and without having issued an RFP?

Joe: And we've only heard about one replacement for the machine oil and the current supply will run out in three days. Let's approve that purchase with the new vendor and write a clause into the contract that gives us an out if the product doesn't work out. We've got to have the oil or the whole production line will shut down.

Vic: I agree with Joe too. Let's move this order up in priority. We can't let the lines shut down. The SmartOil company has been in business for 50 years and deserves a shot at our business. I really think these two orders should be approved.

Janet: How badly can things turn out? Let's place the orders and work with Cynthia on quality specifications when she gets back in two days.

Joe: I don't know about the bulbs but we need the oil now.

Cedric: Okay...

Questions

1. Who is at extreme excitement? How can you tell?

2. If you were Cedric, what would you do and say to get the participants to make a decision?

3. If you were Joe, what would you do and say to get your co-workers to reach agreement on what actions to take?

4. If you were Janet, what would you do and say to get a decision made during this meeting?

Potential Answers

1. Vic Toney, vendor relations specialist, has reached extreme excitement regarding these two orders. You can tell because each time he speaks he is endorsing a go-ahead decision and is supporting the recommended vendors.

2. As meeting leader, Cedric has been in a neutral mindset listening to what team members have to say about the purchases to be made. He needs to get group approvals before the meeting ends. Separating the two decisions is the place to start. "Okay, let's focus on the machine oil purchase first as that is our most critical decision and could shut us down if we don't get more. What concerns does anyone have about approving a SmartOil purchase and placing the express order today?" Then wait for comment. If no one blocks this recommended decision, Cedric can say "Then it's done. Janet, will you please place the order right after this meeting?" Now Cedric needs to handle the second decision, "Now for the meeting room light bulbs. This is a lower priority than the oil, but we need to move it forward too because the facility guys have been asking for better bulbs for more than six months. Is there any reason that we shouldn't order from MeetingElectrics?" Again, wait for comments. If no one blocks the decision, move ahead and place the order. If however, someone or several people block the order, then ask, "What would need to change for us to order from MeetingElectrics?" Or, ask the team, "When can a better vendor be presented for our consideration?" Navigating to a final decision often requires a series of open- and closed-ended questions along with clear defining statements to move the decision discussion to closure.

3. Joe's concern is the machine oil. He can focus on this decision in several ways. He could make a formal motion, "I move that we approve a three-month supply of machine oil be purchased from SmartOil today." Joe could also opt to take a less formal approach and suggest, "I know you all are hesitant to go to a new vendor. But we need the oil to be here so that the lines don't have to shut down. Let's order a three-month supply of machine oil from SmartOil today." Whatever approach Joe takes, he is staying focused on the urgency of the product needed to keep the production line running.

4. Janet's concern has been focused on the meeting room light bulb conversion needs. She's been under pressure for months to move this decision forward. Janet too could make a motion: "I move that we order a one-month supply of the meeting room bulbs from MeetingElectrics and then work with our facility team to see if they are happy with the conversion." Or, she could take the informal route: "Let's place one order with MeetingElectrics for six of our meeting rooms. Then in a month or two we can check with our facility team to see how things are working out." In all cases, as meeting leader, it is Cedric's responsibility to summarize the decisions made and to state which team member is responsible for what actions after this meeting.

Scenario 2—Shifting Extreme Excitement into Recognizing Other Points of View

A person in extreme excitement can get so focused on one point of view that others feel they are not being listened to. Determine what you'd do to enlarge the following conversation before moving to a decision.

JoDean has just made a presentation that included a go-ahead endorsement for changing the company dress code policy to something that allows shorts, flip-flops, and halter tops year round. The ConsulArch company is a business services consulting firm. Everyone in the meeting thinks JoDean is full of unreasonable ideas that he always seems to defend to the end. Let's join the meeting.

SuAnn: You're not listening to the pitfalls of your plan. Dressing like that will detract from our professionalism. We're recognized in our market for our consistent advice and our professionalism.

JoDean: What do you mean? All you ever bring up are the pitfalls.

Bill: Seriously, your idea sounds like great freedom of expression could happen but I don't know that it is a good idea.

JoDean: Why are you all ganging up on this? We are seen as stodgy, out-of-step, and not being current on trends by clients we've lost and by potential clients. We're not hip and we need a change.

Gene: Well maybe there are other ways to address these concerns.

JoDean: Maybe. But we have to start somewhere so let's start here and approve this today.

SuAnn: I don't think so. I'm not going along with this one.

Questions

1. If you were leading this meeting, what would you do and say now?

2. If you were Gene, what could you say next to encourage "other ways" be explored for addressing the concerns JoDean has articulated?

3. What can SuAnn do or say to move herself out of boxed-in and into helping make a decision?

Potential Answers

1. Before the meeting turns into an all out argument, the meeting leader needs to take control of the meeting discussion. Phrases such as the following can work to regain control and move the team to an agreeable next step: "Okay. We're bantering about a lot of ideas, most of which we can't agree upon. So, let's focus on what we can do. What three ideas might be workable?" Or, "We need to reach a decision today. Take a moment individually, without talking, to write down the one idea you think we should pursue." Then wait for everyone to write down one idea. Once you see that each person has an idea that could be shared, say, "Now, let's do a round-the-table sharing of your one-best ideas. Let's see if there are any ideas that match each other or one idea that stands out as actionable." Then, lead the discussion toward a workable action item.

Or, to address each of the ChoiceMark thinkers at the table, you could start with, "We're all coming at this from nearly polar-opposite perspectives. So, everyone write down the one approach that you see as workable and as something you'd support implementing." The breakdown in this team's discussion requires direction giving that leads to an agreement and may ultimately require a move to command-and-control direction giving such as, "Thanks for sharing all of your ideas and suggestions. I'm going to review all of your comments and ideas and make a decision that we'll then implement."

2. Gene has recognized what JoDean's real concerns for the company are. To enlarge the discussion around the real concerns and to encourage new ideas, Gene could use the following approaches: "JoDean, you've brought up some great points about what you are hearing from potential customers. So, let's focus on the concerns. First, what are we doing as a firm that tells people we are stodgy and out of step?" Then wait for team members to discuss this. If people push on making the original decision about the dress code and don't address the real spoken concerns, the firm will likely be hurt by a poor decision. If the team engages in the conversation, improved problem solving and decision making can occur. Once a conversation has begun, Gene can keep expanding the conversation to get to real and viable solutions by asking such questions as "What can we do to become more current from our client's point of view? What resources do we need to shift our behaviors and therefore our client's perceptions? JoDean, what other ideas do you have for overcoming our stale image?"

3. SuAnn's goal is to protect the company's reputation and professionalism. She's boxed herself into a single set of perceptions about how to do this. If she can acknowledge this about herself, she could voice to the group, "Okay. I hear what you are saying that maybe our company is coming across as stale in our market. My real concerns are about our reputation for professionalism. This idea doesn't reflect our professionalism. So, what approaches could we take to become more in tune with trends and be seen for our currency and our professionalism?"

Scenario 3—Gaining Implementation Commitment from Extreme Excitement People

As you read about earlier in this chapter, just because someone is making a decision from the position of extreme excitement doesn't mean that follow-through will occur.

Meeting Leader: Okay. We've generated a lot of ideas today. And we just agreed to build an implementation plan for our decision to add connecting cable production to our existing hardware product line.

Joyce: Right. I'm in project overload right now. Can you get this done without me?

Jim: I guess I can help out. What needs to be done?

Jaclyn: We've been waiting for this decision a long time. I'm surprised you all aren't more excited about finally moving forward. I'm in. I'll help get this done. In fact, I'll check in with accounting to confirm what dollar amount is available for implementation. And, I'll check with training to see when we can roll out the new machine-operator training. Then, I can talk to production to see what their needs are for adding connecting cable manufacturing onto the floor.

JoAnn: I'm pretty swamped but I guess I can fit in some research time on this.

Jacque: We better get with production. This plan will change a lot of their floor space, inventory, and staffing needs. I'm not convinced we should be moving ahead with this without talking to them. Production needs to have input and a final say on this.

Jake: Customers have spoken. We need to add this to our product offerings or we risk losing even our existing sales. We've made the decision to move forward. Let's do that and we can always regroup after we've gotten the next round of planning for implementation done.

Questions

1. As meeting leader in the above meeting, what will you do or say to ensure that successful implementation happens with the team members in extreme excitement?

2. As meeting leader, what could you say to get each team member to commit to some level of implementation?

Potential Answers

1. Jaclyn is the only team member in extreme excitement. In fact, she's so excited about a decision to move forward that she appears to be taking on the entire task of creating an implementation plan. As meeting leader, while still in the meeting, you can say to Jaclyn, "We appreciate your dedication to moving this forward. Each of us has a role in building an implementation plan. So, which three contacts do you most want to make?" Wait for her to narrow her own task list. After she's narrowed it, then ask others, "Who would like to contact the remaining or even other departments that need to be included in the plan discussion?" Again, wait for people to volunteer. If Jaclyn can't narrow her list and if others don't volunteer, as meeting leader it is time to make assignments or to hold one-on-one meetings with team members to find out realistically what each member can do. After the action-commitments have been made, check in with each person who agreed to take action. See what progress is being made and offer your support and assistance to ensure the plan gets built.

2. Ultimately, the meeting leader needs several team members to participate in building the plan. One in-the-meeting approach to securing commitment is to summarize: "Before we adjourn, what plan research have we now committed to?" List the items on a flipchart, whiteboard, or shared technology device. Then ask, "Who is going to lead on each of these items?" Add names to the action list. Include a lead person and supporting names when more than one person volunteers to complete an item. Finally, pin down, "What report-back date should we agree on?" Record the due date for each item and when the report back to this team will be.

Scenario 4—Determining Whether to Stay in Consensus Mode or Shift to Command and Control with People in Extreme Excitement

Sometimes people in extreme excitement work so hard to get others to join them in their excitement that time runs short for making a decision. When a decision is needed in the same meeting that a stalled discussion is occurring, it becomes time to shift to a command decision and recommend implementation. Recall that earlier in this chapter there was a discussion of how people in extreme excitement can look like they are in command-and-control decision mode. How can this meeting moment be moved to decision?

Ray: This is it. We can move ahead and get enough support to have everything done by our next quarterly meeting. Then we can give an update at the executive team's meeting the following month. This is a great decision to make. I hope you'll all help get things done. My team is going to be really glad when we make this decision. They've been waiting for months to have a more creative outlet for their talents. Are you all ready to make a decision and approve a budget?

Rachel: We've spent our entire meeting on this one topic. When will we talk about the other agenda items?

Ron: I agree. All we seem to do in these meetings is talk. We never reach a decision.

Robert: We need to hear from everyone and get their expertise when we make decisions.

Roy: Sure, sure. But I agree with Ron, we never reach a decision.

Reme: Wait. Ray asked us if we are ready to make a decision. Are we?

Rachel: Not if it takes more time. I've got three more urgent decisions that affect my team's ability to get work done in the next two weeks.

Ron: Sure let's make a decision. I say go ahead if my team's time isn't affected. Ray—can your team get this all done without my team?

Ray: You bet. They are ready and eager.

Roy: Okay. But my team will be affected and we don't have any extra time or resources to commit. I'm not willing to pull my team off of their current projects. So, I'm not in favor of this.

Questions

1. Which team members are in extreme excitement?

2. As the meeting leader of this chaotic meeting, how will you step in and move the team to a decision?

3. If you are Reme, how would you help the meeting leader move the talk to a decision?

Potential Answers

1. Ray and only Ray is in extreme excitement. He has hinted that the rest of his team members are also excited about taking on the new project.

2. This group needs a clear decision. Consensus is not working. Each team member seems headed in a different direction and the time frame for making a decision really is now, in this meeting. As meeting leader, you can move the team to action with a sequence of questions and statements: "You're all right. We need a decision. And we need a decision that allows our normal work to continue while taking on a creative new project that can add to our revenue. What is one good thing that can come out of moving ahead with this decision?" Now wait to hear from each person at the table. Record the ideas on a flipchart or in the minutes. "So, there are some good things that can come out of moving ahead with the decision. Each of your teams has had an opportunity to pursue new projects over the last few years and Ray's team hasn't. His team is due for an opportunity to be creative and still add to our bottom line. So, I'll give Ray's team the opportunity to research and pull together a budget and an implementation plan. Ray, you need to report back these items to this team in two weeks so that you can get more buy-in from this team about rolling out your plan. In the meantime, for the next two weeks, each of your work will go ahead without any changes."

3. Reme was able to easily identify the requested decision point and to urge the group to make a decision. His contributions to move the group to a final decision could include, "Let's make a decision so Ray and his team know how to proceed," or, "Ray, can you bring a budget proposal to our next meeting so we know just how big this project is? Without that information the rest of us are having a hard time committing to the decision."

Whenever you find yourself or others in extreme excitement, pause to listen to multiple points of view. Individuals and teams working together at the extreme excitement level of consensus can achieve incredible, creative, and above-average results. When reaching extreme excitement, some individuals and teams remain fractured and have difficulty achieving the agreed-upon outcomes. The key is to use ChoiceMarks language during and after decision making in order to ensure best-possible decisions are made and implemented.

Chapter Summary

I've got it. When I reach extreme excitement my passion is great, so great in fact that I can become more effective by realizing that everyone is not likely at my same level of excitement. Improving my decision making, question asking, and listening skills will help in every ChoiceMark consensus stage I reach. If I'm not in extreme excitement, I also can use questions from this chapter to expand a conversation, move it to a decision, and encourage implementation.

Working with Engaged Enthusiasm

Engaged Enthusiasm, It's All Shades of Degree

The first iteration of ChoiceMarks included the language Excitement, instead of Engaged Enthusiasm. While introducing the model to a variety of business sectors and trade groups, I discovered a niche aversion to the word excitement. Who objected? The engineer and scientific communities suggested that "being engaged" and "enthusiasm" were better terms than the word "excitement." As a result, this stage of consensus commitment became "engaged enthusiasm." What is most interesting is that the words engaged, enthusiastic, and excited are really all shades or degrees of being excited. So engaged enthusiasm represents a degree of consensus that includes commitment to action yet not at the level of heightened passion, drive, and excitement of the person or team in extreme excitement. The reality when working with groups is that engaged enthusiasm is most likely to be the state of consensus for action. At this level of consensus, a large enough part of the team will engage to move the decision forward and ensure that follow-through occurs.

Engaged enthusiasm is recognizable because heads nod in agreement and any questions asked focus on how things will get done rather than on why things can't get done. One step to many steps removed from the extreme passion of extreme excitement, engaged enthusiasm is still also dedicated to an affirmative decision being made so that implementation for change can occur. Anyone who has volunteered to serve on a team, task force, committee, or board has reached a level of engaged enthusiasm or extreme excitement. At the other five stages of consensus, individuals are unlikely to volunteer their services. Reaching at least engaged enthusiasm before volunteering can happen for anyone once the point or points of interest for a project have been found.

When Individuals Reach Engaged Enthusiasm

Individuals reach engaged enthusiasm when they have a belief in the project and a trust that it can be achieved. Just as personal interest, study or experience can fuel the energies of someone in extreme excitement, the same can be said for someone in engaged enthusiasm. General interest in a project, clarity about how the project can help the organization, or hopes for organizational improvement and successes also can fuel the energies and commitment of someone in engaged enthusiasm. Whatever its source, engaged enthusiasm is characterized by commitment to an affirmative decision and its implementation, and by occasional challenges with listening to other points of view.

When you reach engaged enthusiasm, listening can become a challenge. Ask what you are listening for. For instance, are you listening for data to support your point of view or listening for divergent points of view? Are you listening for all the upsides, pros, and affirmations, or for some of the downsides, cons, and project challenges too? When you ask what you are truly open to hearing, you are engaged in discernment. To be discerning means to recognize and understand differences and to show insight and understanding about a topic or discussion and where it needs to head in order for decisions to be made. While in engaged enthusiasm, listen for information that supports your own viewpoints and conclusions. Then listen for opposing points of view to discern how a decision and implementation plan can be improved. Finally, listen for information that helps you discern what others are thinking and what ChoiceMark location they are communicating from. By recognizing others' ChoiceMark stages of consensus, you'll be better able to involve them in the problem-solving and decision-making discussion.

Groups Don't Need to Reach Unanimous Engaged Enthusiasm to Make Decisions

In the workplace, decision making is not usually about right and wrong (which would be a discussion of ethics and other books address this topic in depth). In most workplaces, decision making is more often about looking at all of the options and selecting the best-possible option for moving forward. When the majority of a team's members reach engaged enthusiasm during decision making, the team is more likely to experience full and successful implementation. Typically a team can successfully implement a decision when members reach neutral, engaged enthusiasm, and extreme excitement. A mixture of the ChoiceMark consensus stages is most typical during day-to-day decision making.

Recall the example given in Chapter 4, in which many board members were pushing me to move to extreme excitement. I stayed in neutral, while others were in engaged enthusiasm and committed to the fund raising plans implementation. The point is that not everyone on a team has to reach the same stage of consensus for a decision to be made. However, it is critical that no one or no team subset ends up working against or standing in the way of a team's decision. When this happens, the members of a team working against implementation can undermine and even destroy the success of the implementation. Again, decisions can be made and successfully implemented even when team members are in several if not all stages of the ChoiceMarks continuum.

Questions to Ask When You Are in Engaged Enthusiasm

When you are the person in engaged enthusiasm and ready to move to implementation, consider all information that will help improve the decision and its implementation, even if that information seems to be in opposition to the decision at hand. Ask any of the following questions or inviting sentences in order to uncover as much helpful information as possible for decision making and implementation.

- What experiences have you had with this situation?
- What can you tell us about making sure implementation is successful?
- When has our company tried this in the past? How did things go?
- How can this be improved?
- How can we best implement this decision?
- How much information can you share without violating any confidentiality agreements?
- Which resources will we need to implement the decision successfully?
- Who else can help us build our implementation plan?
- Where can we look for lessons from similar situations?
- What time frames seem realistic to you?

Questions to Ask When Others Are in Engaged Enthusiasm

When someone else is entrenched in engaged enthusiasm, the ability to listen to opposing points of view can be diminished. As a result, it is important to acknowledge the excitement and enthusiasm this person has. Then, work to engage the person in a conversation that enlarges the discussion. Your questions and ideas may change the decision outcome. If the decision outcome is not changed by your input, at least the discussion included potential pitfalls. You can seek more information from or suggest new angles of discussion with someone in engaged enthusiasm by asking questions or making information invitations such as the following:

- What has convinced you that this is the best course of action?
- What information can you share with us that might persuade us to your point of view?
- Where have you seen this work successfully?
- What leads you to this conclusion?
- What is your vision for implementing this decision?
- Which subject matter experts will need to review our plans?
- Where will we find the resources and staffing to accomplish this?
- When is it realistic to move ahead with this plan?
- What timeline do you envision as being realistic?

Just Because Someone Reached Engaged Enthusiasm, Don't Expect Something to Get Done

While individuals in engaged enthusiasm are most likely to help achieve the implementation of a decision, just because they are here, don't expect everything to get done. The same end-of-meeting strategies used with people in extreme excitement work with individuals in engaged enthusiasm. Before a decision-making meeting ends, be sure to secure commitment for follow-up actions and decision implementation. Also before the end of every meeting, clearly state who is responsible for getting what done and by what deadline. Then, encourage the engaged enthusiasm team members to achieve the result and to let you know if any help or resources are needed along the way. Use phrases such as, "Thanks for taking this on. Let us know what you want help with along the way."

To ensure decision implementation, check in periodically on the progress toward the agreed-upon results. People in an engaged enthusiasm stage can sometimes hit frustrations and disappointments that prevent achievement of the original agreed-upon outcomes. On the other hand, they can move ahead so eagerly that needed input is not gathered along the way to ensure ongoing buy-in and follow-through. On the positive side, teams in engaged enthusiasm that have gathered critical input along the way can achieve above-average results and creativity during implementation. Additional between-meeting implementation and follow-through can be invited by using the same phrases as used to check in with people in extreme excitement: "Just checking in; how are things going? Any problems? Any challenges coming up that we need to address? Let me know if you need anything to get this done. Have you encountered any roadblocks? What can we do to overcome the roadblocks? What successes are you having?" Remember to really pause and listen. When help is most needed is often the time when people are most reluctant to speak up.

Getting Someone to Engaged Enthusiasm

Teams do not have to unanimously reach engaged enthusiasm in order to make decisions. However, individuals in engaged enthusiasm are more likely to follow through on implementation of decision action items. Someone in extreme excitement doesn't need to be coached to engaged enthusiasm, rather the extreme excitement person needs coaching and cheering that ensures implementation occurs. Someone in neutral can be invited to engaged enthusiasm to increase the likelihood of follow-through. When a person is in neutral, the communication is, "Tell me more about why this is such a good idea, and why I should participate in getting it done." As a result, you can share information about why the decision and the implementation plans are in fact good ideas. You can invite input from the person or people in neutral to learn and discern what else in the discussed plan can be improved. When engaging people in a neutral stage of consensus in the problem-solving discussion, you are more likely to get participation in the implementation and perhaps move them to a level of engaged enthusiasm that helps to ensure successful implementation.

When working with individuals in the boxed-in and anti-survival points of view and stages of consensus, remember that their messages are telling you, "We don't think this will work." In order to invite movement to a neutral or engaged enthusiasm point of view, individual concerns must be addressed and overcome before boxed-in and anti-survival will consider moving to neutral, let alone to engaged enthusiasm. And yes, it really is possible to hear out the boxed-in and anti-survival points of view, to address their concerns, and include specific elements for overcoming the concerns in the implementation plan such that mindsets can shift to engaged enthusiasm. You've likely heard the phrase, "Our biggest opponents are now our biggest supporters." This phrase is an example of moving boxed-in and anti-survival thinkers to engaged enthusiasm and even extreme excitement.

With this added information about engaged enthusiasm, you are ready to continue practice recognizing the ChoiceMark decision points and selecting language that you can use to move decision discussions forward to an actual decision. Identify discussion decision points and crafting language that would work in each scenario to move the team toward a decision. These practices are designed for you to build your skills and confidence as a decision maker, as a team leader, and as a team member.

ChoiceMark Practices

Read through each scenario. Watch for decision point language and signals. Respond to the questions at the end of each scenario. Also identify which of the four scenarios are similar to situations you've experienced. Then consider how you can now go back and handle your own decision situations with greater effectiveness.

Scenario 1—Recognizing Engaged Enthusiasm in Action

You'll recognize this first scenario from Chapter 4. However, the meeting has progressed and now, the person in engaged enthusiasm has a chance to move the team to a decision. Each Thursday morning, the Alpharet Company purchasing department continues to hold a staff meeting for the purpose of identifying new products needed by the company, updating request for proposal (RFP) statuses, and updating back-ordered products that may require finding new suppliers. Cedric Fredricksen is the meeting leader and is also the director for the purchasing department. The attendees at the meeting include: Joe Anderson, purchasing specialist; Janet Hernandez, purchasing specialist; Fred Alverez, RFP issuing agent; and Vic Toney, vendor relations specialist. Absent from the last meeting but present this time is Cynthia Thorngaard, who is the quality control specialist. The staff meeting discussions have progressed. The last meeting's decision to buy machine oil was implemented and the manufacturing supervisors seem fine with the product and its quality. However, a final decision on the new meeting room light bulbs still has not been reached. Twenty minutes into another one hour meeting no decisions have been reached and there are still four decision items remaining on the agenda. Nearly everyone, including meeting leader Cedric, is frustrated.

Cedric: Okay. Last meeting we took action on the machine oil and it seems to be working out. We've spent another twenty minutes debating the light bulbs. We need to make a decision today and get this off of our to-do list. I appreciate all of the input you have each given.

Janet: I still think we have enough information to go with MeetingElectrics for the light bulbs.

Vic: And I still agree with Janet. Remember, I've met with MeetingElectrics' president several times in the last six months. They really want our business and I think they'll work hard to meet our needs and keep our business. Let's approve the order already.

Fred: We could issue an RFP. I worked one up after our last meeting. However, I still want Cynthia's input on the quality and safety standards that need to be in the RFP.

Joe: I don't have input on this one.

Vic: Well, what do we need Cynthia? I really think the RFP should be issued and that we should lean toward MeetingElectrics as our vendor.

Cynthia: We'll need to know the safety ratings for the bulbs; the number of hours they typically last; the disposal process and whether we have to dispose of the bulbs or whether the vendor will; the installation process; and failure rate per 100 bulbs. Fred, can you write these into specifications in the RFP that match our other lighting specifications?

Fred: Sure.

Janet: Seems like an awful lot of details. Do we really need to be so picky? The order is just for meeting room light bulbs.

Cynthia and Fred in unison: Yes!

Fred: If we aren't specific enough, we'll end up with so many new vendors thinking they can fill our needs that we'll have too many proposals to sort through.

Cedric: Okay.

Questions

1. Who is at engaged enthusiasm? How can you tell?

2. If you were Cedric what would you do and say to get the participants to make a decision?

3. If you were Cynthia, what would you do and say to get your co-workers to reach agreement on what actions to take?

4. If you were Janet, what would you do and say to get a decision made during this meeting?

Potential Answers

1. Janet is in engaged enthusiasm. She is ready for a decision to be made, supports Vic's still in extreme excitement, and wants implementation to occur as soon as possible.

2. As meeting leader, Cedric has been in a neutral mindset listening to what team members have to say about the RFP needs and the desires of Vic and Janet to just approve MeetingElectrics. Still in team-oriented mode, he needs to get group approval to issue the RFP before the meeting ends. Cedric could start with, "Cynthia will you and Fred get together to finalize the details for the RFP? Then, go ahead and issue the RFP with a submission deadline two weeks from now. That way Janet can get back to the facility team to let them know we are in process with this."

3. Cynthia can suggest any of the following approaches: "Fred and I can get together to finalize a RFP that narrows the field of potential suppliers," or, "I'll email Fred the specifications we need to have met for light bulbs in our meeting rooms. Then he can craft the RFP," or, taking a less action-oriented approach, Cynthia could defer direction giving to Cedric: "Cedric, what would you have me do? You know my specification writing to-do list is long right now, and I didn't think the light bulbs were a high priority yet."

4. Janet's concern has been focused on the meeting room light bulb conversion needs. She's been under pressure for months to move this decision forward so she's at engaged enthusiasm and wants to get this item off of her to-do list. Because a decision to buy still isn't in order, Janet could choose to formalize her request by saying, "I suggest we get the RFP written and issued in the next week with a deadline of the following week so that we can get this off our to-do lists and onto our regular vendor purchasing database." Regardless of which team member offers the move-forward solution, in all cases it is Cedric the meeting leader's responsibility to summarize the decisions made and to state which team member is responsible for what actions after this meeting and by what deadlines.

Scenario 2—Shifting Engaged Enthusiasm into Recognizing Other Points of View

A person in engaged enthusiasm can get so focused on the get-it-done point of view that others feel they are not being listened to. Even people in neutral can feel frustrated about not being heard. Determine what you'd do to enlarge the following conversation before moving to a decision.

The meeting leader is Ernie Burdick, team leader of the budget preparation team for the marketing department. Meeting participants include Kraig Andersen, Mary Poels, Joe Johnson, and Marcia Gladwell, each of whom works in the marketing department. The current budget preparation meeting's purpose is to reach agreement on dollar amounts for every line item in the departments' two-year budget projection.

Ernie: We are two weeks out from having to submit our department's two-year budget to the executive team for approvals. Today we need to reach agreement on every line item in this budget.

Kraig: I'm ready.

Mary: Well, I haven't gotten any of the input the advertising unit promised me for this meeting.

Kraig: Okay, then why don't we start with what we do have?

Ernie: We can do that...

Joe: Sure, we've got some budget inputs. We can look at the product packaging, branding and logos, and the internet teams budgets.

Mary: Without the advertising projections we can't complete their line items.

Kraig: That's okay. Get them this week and we can finalize them in next week's meeting.

Marcia: Let's focus on what we can do today.

Kraig: That's right, let's dive in and get some decisions made.

Ernie: Let's.

Questions

1. If you were leading this meeting, what would you do and say now?

2. Which team member is in engaged enthusiasm? How can he contribute to getting Mary out of boxed-in?

3. What can Marcia, who appears to be in neutral, do or say to move the team to start the decision making discussion?

Potential Answers

1. As Ernie is the meeting leader, he has the responsibility to get the engaged enthusiasm of Kraig and the boxed-in thinking of Mary as well as Marcia's neutral approach to focus on what can be done today. Deadlines are near and many line items in the budget need to be set for submission to the executive team. Ernie could offer any of the following questions to the meeting group to prompt action. "Which set of line items should we focus on first? How about the internet team's data?" or, "Let's focus on the brands and logo line items. They have the fewest line items for review and that will get us moving," or, "Kraig, you're pretty engaged with this project. Which area do you recommend we begin with?" Whatever approach Ernie takes, the key is to get the team focused on what they can do right now in this meeting.

2. Kraig is in engaged enthusiasm. He is "ready" and is consistently offering suggestions for moving forward. If Kraig is listening with discernment, rather than getting frustrated with Mary, he will be able to recognize her boxed-in thinking and invite her to at least move to neutral so the team can go ahead with the line item input they do have. Kraig could say, "Mary, I hear your frustration about the missing information. What can the rest of us do to help get that information for the next meeting?" Then, Kraig and all of the team members need to wait for Mary to reply. Mary might ask for help, or she might say she'll get with the right people to get the input. Either way, the next step is to focus on what can be done today. Kraig can then suggest, "Great, next week we'll look at their input. Today, let's start with the product packaging input as they've asked for big increases."

3. Because Marcia appears to be approaching the discussion from a neutral point of view, she can be a bridge between Mary's boxed-in thinking and Kraig's engaged enthusiasm. Marcia could contribute to the conversation with phrases such as, "Why don't we start with what we have?" or, "How about starting with the product packaging input? They've got the biggest year-over-year changes in their requests."

Scenario 3—Gaining Implementation Commitment from Engaged Enthusiasm People

Just because someone is making a decision from the position of engaged enthusiasm doesn't mean that follow-through will occur. While it is more likely that follow-through will occur, obstacles can derail the implementation process. The following team meeting has just discovered that the team members most committed to implementation after the decision-making meeting three weeks ago have run into an obstacle that threatens to prevent implementation. What would you do to regain the commitment of the engaged enthusiasm team members?

Meeting Leader: Okay, we've run into some obstacles. Three weeks ago we made a commitment to implement a new workflow to reduce the amount of paperwork we are handling each day. Some of the ideas for reduction are working and no one has complained of missing the documents. However, we have had a few complaints from the risk management and insurance departments.

George: That's for sure. Risk management has come down hard on me and I was skeptical of the success of the paper reduction idea in the first place.

Gerry: Well, most of the improvements are being met with appreciation.

Meeting Leader: Gerry, that's true. However, these two department's frustrations and concerns are important to address. We can't create problems for some departments while working to increase efficiencies for the whole company.

Georgia: Three weeks ago, I was really optimistic about our plans for improvement. And Gerry is right, most things are going well. However, I've spent several hours with George trying to come up with solutions for risk management's concerns and everything we suggest to them is met with "no, we still need the paper." So we need to figure out a new solution for them.

Geoff: I was optimistic too, and my liaison in the insurance department is saying that they need a much longer paper trail than what we came up with three weeks ago. Maybe we need to scrap the new approach and go back to the old way of doing things.

Meeting Leader: Okay, before we give up . . .

Questions

1. Which team members were clearly in engaged enthusiasm at some point in the discussions?

2. As meeting leader in the above meeting, what will you do or say to regain the commitment of the team members in engaged enthusiasm?

3. As meeting leader, what could you say to get each team member to commit to some level of implementation?

Potential Answers

1. Georgia and Geoff have indicated that they were in engaged enthusiasm.

2. The Meeting Leader can continue, "Okay, before we give up, let's focus on what complaints the insurance department is expressing and explore what we can do to address their concerns," or, "Okay, before we give up, George, what demands is the risk management department making?" Uncovering where the problems are will allow new problem solving to occur and will invite those engaged

in solution implementation to stay committed to achieving the goal of reduced paperwork.

3. Ultimately, the meeting leader needs all of the team members to participate in solving the risk management and insurance problems. For instance, during the meeting, the meeting leader can secure commitment by inviting team members to summarize where the problems are: "What are the main complaints from the risk management department?" List the items of concern on a flipchart, whiteboard, or shared technology device. Then ask: "What can be done to overcome each concern?" Add the potential solutions to the list and then ask, "How should we proceed to solve the risk management team's concerns?" Then listen for suggestions. Before the meeting ends, summarize who is going to do what to follow up on the potential solutions. Finally, pin down "What report-back date should we agree on?" Record the due-date for each action item.

Scenario 4—Determining Whether to Stay in Consensus Mode or Shift to Command and Control with People in Engaged Enthusiasm

Sometimes people in engaged enthusiasm gain such momentum for a decision that individuals in boxed-in and anti-survival decide to work against the decision. When time runs short for making a decision, the meeting leader or a team member needs to focus the group on making a decision. Especially when a decision is needed in the same meeting that the stalling discussion is occurring. Shifting to a command decision and recommending implementation is sometimes the most expedient course of action. How can this meeting moment be moved to decision?

Meeting Leader Isabelle: We need to finalize the implementation plan for the decision we made three weeks ago.

Juanita: We're set for implementation starting next Monday. The affected departments have signed off on the changes and seem ready, even excited about most of the changes.

Jorge: I have some concerns about the direction you all are headed.

Vincent: This is not the direction to head. You all are not paying attention to the reasons this won't work. The areas of concern probably fall into the discussion areas that you are not hearing comments on from the affected departments.

MaryAnn: Yes, we've listened to all of the reasons it won't work and offered ideas for overcoming the challenges. Now we need to move ahead.

Jorge: I'm not going to stand in your way, but I do think you are going to run into serious challenges.

Vincent: And, I'm telling you that this won't work.

Victoria: Okay, we've heard that.

Vincent: Seriously, don't go ahead with this action plan for implementation. Someone will get hurt.

Michael: Can't we move forward and then address the challenges or trouble spots as they arise?

Victoria: Okay. Really, we've heard your concerns, the departments are not complaining, and we need to move forward. Monday is just days away.

Questions

1. Which team members are in engaged enthusiasm?

2. As the meeting leader of this going-nowhere meeting, how will you step in and move the team to a decision?

3. If you are Victoria, how would you help the meeting leader move the talk to a decision?

Potential Answers

1. Juanita, MaryAnn, and Victoria appear to be in engaged enthusiasm. Each of them is ready to move forward with the implementation plan.

2. In this meeting, each point of view in the ChoiceMarks continuum of coming to consensus needs to be acknowledged and then invited to move to a problem-solving mindset. Right now, each meeting participant is locked into their own point of view. The meeting leader can move to a command-and-control direction giving approach: "We need to focus on what we can do. Victoria has made the point that implementation is already set for Monday. Will moving ahead hurt anyone or harm our production?" If someone says "yes," ask them to show to whom and how harm will occur, then determine whether a "stop-the-implementation" decision is now in order and say this to the group. If no one offers any examples of hurt or harm occurring, then state, "We are going to help each affected department roll out the changes on Monday. We'll let the new systems run for the entire week and next Friday we'll meet to discuss what if any refinements are needed."

3. Victoria can support the move to a decision by asking for direction. She might say: "Give us some direction. We're too close to implementation to keep rehashing our decision." Or she might turn to the meeting leader and say, "You decide and tell us what you want done."

Action Is Demanded

Whatever the challenge to a decision-making process, having at least one person in engaged enthusiasm helps a team focus on how a positive decision can be made and what can be done to accomplish successful implementation. Regardless of the mindsets and stages of consensus that a team ends up having, action is demanded. Meetings are held for discussions to occur that move the organization forward. Any time a meeting group gets stuck, a meeting leader or the meeting participants themselves need to find the language that will move the group to a decision. The discussion strengths of an engaged enthusiasm person include looking for can-do solutions, listening for ideas that will solve problems, and a willingness to personally commit to implementing solutions.

Chapter Summary

Okay, so when I'm in engaged enthusiasm, I need to do a better job of listening to other points of view. I will also focus on better discerning whether the team can move ahead successfully without every member committing to positive action. I now know that decisions can be made and follow-up action can occur even without some team members, as long as they don't sabotage the project. And if I'm not the person in engaged enthusiasm, I now know how to expand the decision conversation to get other points of view considered before a decision is made. Reaching at least a moderate level of engaged enthusiasm tends to lead to improved decision implementation and follow-through.

CHAPTER **6**

Moving Ahead with Neutral

Nothing Beats Neutral—Everything Beats Neutral

Neutral can be defined as a position of disengagement. This makes sense in the shades-of-degree consensus discussion because we started with Extreme Excitement and downshifted to a still committed to, or in favor of, level of engaged enthusiasm. After two levels of engagement comes one level of disengagement. Being disengaged or unattached to an outcome can open the discussion to critical question asking and to supportive seeking of information that contributes to best-possible decision making. Neutral can also be defined as not being engaged on either side of a discussion or an issue. In other words, sitting in the middle can contribute to an ability to listen to all points of view before reaching a decision. Neutral can also mean being non-committal. This can be a problem when clear decisions are needed. When being neutral creates an individual or team state of indecisiveness, this state of waffling can hurt the organization because critical deadlines are missed, problems fail to be solved in a timely manner, and cost increases resulting from indecision causing budget over-runs which can all create problems throughout an organization.

On the other hand, nothing beats neutral because having an ability to listen to all points of view before making a decision can lead to improved decision making on the part of individuals and teams. The two levels of consensus on either side of neutral incline listeners to specific points of view: Extreme excitement listens for information supporting the decision and a similar level of passion and commitment; engaged enthusiasm listens for information supporting the decision and commitment to the action; boxed-in listens for opposing information that works against the decision; and anti-survival listens for opposing information that will create a "no" or "don't do it" agreement at the end of a decision discussion. Neutral can gather information from all four stages of ChoiceMark consensus and lead others to seeing multiple points of view. Being neutral can be an asset to the team and to a decision making process.

However, when individuals stay in neutral, entire teams can end up in neutral. When this happens, no decisions get made and no follow up action occurs. In this case, everything beats neutral. Like the waffler-style decision makers, people in neutral are perceived as indecisive and uncommitted. While everyone else has a clear opinion, for or against the decision, sitting in neutral can also create levels of disengagement that range from "I don't care, go ahead without me" to "I'm quitting." The challenge with the "I'm quitting" outlook is that it too has a range that goes from "I'm here in the room but I've quit and I'm not giving you any ideas" to "I'm quitting the team, or even my job and this company." In the end, every decision discussion by definition must result in a decision regarding how to move forward or how to bring an end to further action.

Sometimes neutral is the best you can hope for. When a team can't come to consensus against a decision or in favor of a decision, focus on getting individuals to neutral through the use of the ChoiceMark discussion language. Reaching neutral means that individuals have agreed not to stand in the way of those individuals who want to move forward with a decision and its implementation. In other words, individuals in neutral are saying "we won't stand in your way, nor will we help you get it done." In this come-to-consensus approach, those who want to move forward can and those not committed to action on the immediate decision can commit to future decisions.

Net-neutral: this is what opposing attorneys involved in selecting jurors are looking for. In a trial, attorneys are looking for impartial jurors, people who will be neutral enough to listen to the facts and information presented before reaching a conclusion. The attorney for a defendant is looking for jurors willing to listen to reasons the defendant is not guilty, to let the defendant be not-guilty until proven otherwise, and to even find reasons the defendant is not guilty. The prosecuting attorney working to get the defendant convicted or found guilty is looking for jurors willing to listen to reasons the defendant is guilty and to lean toward finding the defendant guilty. All of which means that at the end of selecting jurors, and before a trial begins, the jury should be net-neutral about a person's guilt. When taking a juror position, people are sworn to disregard their prejudices and follow the judge's instructions in order to reach a verdict. Jurors are also encouraged to keep an open mind. Of course by the end of hearing testimony and presentations the jurors have gathered information to take into the jury deliberation room that will be used to make a guilty or not-guilty decision or series of decisions based on the judge's instructions about what the jury must reach a decision upon. Once in the jury room, a foreperson presides over the deliberations and ensures that each person has a chance to express his views and opinions. Most jury decisions require a unanimous vote meaning that every person must vote the same way. And in some cases, agreement by a specified majority of jurors serves as the verdict. Jury deliberations to reach the verdict (decision) are the last stages of the trial process. The process of getting to a unanimous vote definitely includes extended conversation, discussion and debate. This is where the Choice-Marks tool becomes useful.

In the third year of working with the ChoiceMarks consensus tool, several people independently said "this would have helped our jury make a decision." As it happened, both people had served on different juries that experienced difficulty reaching a decision. Of course all kinds of reasons for the difficulties may have existed. However, at the very least, having a decision discussion tool like ChoiceMarks might have helped the jury members reach a decision in a less painful and more timely manner. As a result of the enthusiastic comments about applying ChoiceMarks to jury duty, I began researching the jury deliberation process. The insights from a variety of juror hand-books and guides, as well as language provided for judges to use when giving instructions to a jury are immediately relevant to daily business decision making discussions.

Some of the language used to provide guidance to jurors just before they begin to deliberate is applicable to workplace teams too. For instance, the manuals that guide judicial conduct and language offer that a judge might say: "It is your duty to find the facts from all the evidence in the case. To those facts you will apply the law as I give it to you. You must follow the law as I give it to you whether you agree with it or not. You must not be influenced by any personal likes or dislikes, opinions, prejudices, or sympathy. That means that you must decide the case solely on the evidence before you. You will recall that you took an oath promising to do so at the beginning of the case." Some of this language is occasionally even heard on courtroom television shows and series. In daily organization workplaces, this guidance becomes "You may or may not like what is being presented. Separate out your biases and determine what will be best for our organization."

Further language that a judge can use to give instructions to a jury is also applicable to daily decision making. A judge can say: "When you begin your deliberations, first elect one member of the jury as your presiding juror. That person will preside over the deliberations. He or she will also speak for you here in court. You will then discuss the case with your fellow jurors to reach agreement. Your verdict must be unanimous. Each of you must decide the case for yourself. You should reach a decision only after you have considered all of the evidence, discussed it fully with the other jurors, and listened to the views of your fellow jurors. Do not be afraid to change your opinion if the whole of the discussion persuades you that you should. Do not come to a decision simply because other jurors think it is right. It is important that you attempt to reach a unanimous verdict but, of course, only if each of you can do so after having made your own conscientious decision. Do not change an honest belief about the weight and effect of the evidence simply to reach a verdict."

This language practically provides the structure for decision discussion meetings in our workplaces too. At the start, have someone to preside over or chair the meeting. Then, have a discussion that reflects the information and evidence presented and "discuss it fully." Be open to changing your mind if the discussion persuades you to do so. The level of consensus that must be reached by a jury is that all jurors must agree to the verdict. In our workplaces, on occasion everyone agrees on the same decision. And the last two sentences of guiding language prompt a decision but a decision that is based on an "honest" look at the evidence and "the weight and effect of the evidence." This honest look is reminiscent of the "intellectually honest" trait that General Brooks spoke to in Chapter 2.

Juries sometimes deadlock and are unable to make a decision. Teams and decision units sometimes reach a stalemate that prevents a clear decision from being made. In the case of a judge hearing from a jury about a deadlock, the following language can be used to remind jurors that a guilty or not-guilty decision must be reached. Here is one sentence from the longer paragraphs of language that can be used to prompt jurors to a decision; it is also from the manuals that provide judges with courtroom language: "During your deliberations, you should not hesitate to reexamine your own views and change your opinion if you become persuaded that it is wrong." In daily decision making discussions, the ability to listen with an open enough mind to be able to make decisions and to willingly change an opinion comes from listening with a neutral mindset.

In a jury deliberation, the ChoiceMark continuum still fits. The individual stages of ChoiceMarks might be renamed, but the lines of discussion and question asking are parallel. Extreme excitement corresponds to "definitely not guilty." Engaged enthusiasm corresponds with "probably not guilty." Neutral stays neutral, or not sure of what verdict is correct. Boxed-in corresponds with "probably guilty." And anti-survival ironically corresponds with "definitely guilty." Any jury decision on either side of neutral of course must be "beyond a reasonable doubt."

While juries are asked to reach clear guilty or not-guilty verdicts, our day-to-day work environments have much more flexibility in decision making, sometimes to the detriment of the decision and the organization. With too many team members in neutral, implementation is not as likely to be successful. When governmental and other workplace committees and teams meet, decision making that appears net-neutral can usually be broken into three groups of thinking: those in favor, those in neutral and those against the decision. Being against the final result of a decision can include the voicing of positions not held by the majority. The positions not held by the majority of a group's members are referred to as minority positions. Particularly in government meetings of elected officials those holding minority positions will write a minority report to put their position onto the record or into the minutes to show that opposing points of view were voiced to those holding the majority position. In non-government workplaces, the minority position can be recorded in the minutes document to reflect concerns and opposing points of view that were taken into consideration while reaching a decision.

When Individuals Reach Neutral

In the ChoiceMarks stages of consensus, when someone reaches neutral it can be both good and bad. Neutral is a good stage when a person was previously in the mindset of boxed-in or anti-survival and has had their concerns addressed sufficiently to move them into neutral. On the other hand neutral becomes a bad stage when a person or a team previously committed to action at the engaged enthusiasm or extreme excitement stages shifts to neutral due to a loss of confidence in outcomes. The best case of being in neutral is being open to multiple points of view, being able to enlarge conversations without creating a bias, and finally being able to lead a group to best-possible decision making.

Groups Don't Need to Reach Neutral to Make Decisions

Decisions can be reached at any stage of the ChoiceMarks continuum. When at neutral, individuals will either listen to multiple points of view or sometimes will stop listening altogether due to a lack of interest in the decision under discussion. However if an entire team is in neutral, the challenge is to make a decision at all. In other words, getting everyone on the team to neutral very likely won't help the team to make a decision. When an entire team is in neutral, decisions usually die due to a lack of interest in seeing a problem solved or in making a decision. Therefore, striving for everyone to be in neutral doesn't help decisions get made. The times that striving for neutral can help are twofold. First, when boxed-in and anti-survival thinkers are standing in the way of making a positive do-it decision, getting individuals to neutral can help the team make an affirmative decision. Secondly, when extreme excitement and engaged enthusiasm thinkers are standing in the way of making an appropriate don't-do-it decision, getting individuals to neutral can help the team make the best-possible decision.

Questions to Ask When You Are in Neutral

Because your strength is listening to multiple points of view, others will typically perceive your question-asking as non-threatening. Go ahead and ask questions that can lead the group to making a decision. Because you are in neutral you can ask questions on both sides of neutral to uncover relevant information that can improve the final decision. The following list of questions and phrases gives you a starting place.

- What leads you to believe this won't work?
- What leads you to believe this will work?
- Why should anyone feeling boxed-in or in anti-survival shift their positions?

- Why should team members in engaged enthusiasm or in extreme excitement shift their positions?
- How can we find a middle ground?
- What decision could work for everyone?
- What information do we still need in order to make this decision?
- What can you share that could persuade me to your point of view?
- Where can we go to get the information we need to make a decision one way or the other?
- When does the decision absolutely have to be made?
- What deadlines can we negotiate?

Questions to Ask When Others Are in Neutral

When someone is in neutral, the message to the rest of the team is "you haven't provided me with enough information to move me out of my neutral position. Give me a compelling reason to shift one way or the other." In order to encourage a move out of neutral, the following questions or phrases can be used.

- What questions do you have?
- What expertise or insight do you have on this?
- Who else should we be consulting with to get accurate information?
- Tell us what other information you'd like.
- Is this project one you'd be willing to participate in?
- What element of this decision might you help us implement?
- When will your project load have an opening that would allow your participation on this project?
- Where would you suggest we go to gather more information that might change our approach?
- Do you know of anyone or any teams that we can go to for insight? Who?

Just Because Someone Reached Neutral, Don't Expect Something to Get Done

As stated earlier in this chapter, an entire team in neutral leads to inaction. When an individual is in neutral, it is unlikely that a commitment to action will follow. The tendency for people who stay in neutral is not to block action and not to participate in decision implementation. So if you really need the skills and expertise of someone in neutral, you'll have an opportunity to practice your communication and persuasion skills. To inspire people who are in neutral to a level of action, look for the elements of the decision that the people in neutral are likely to have an interest in and a willingness to help get things accomplished. Focus on what the individual's expertise, experience, and skill sets are and work to discover elements of the project action list that the person will commit to.

Also stated earlier in this chapter, "sometimes neutral is the best you can hope for." When some team members are in neutral and are committed to not blocking and not undermining forward-moving implementation actions, it is okay to move ahead. When team members who are neutral are willing to commit to implementation of some elements of the decision, and as long as no one blocks the decision, it is okay to move ahead. Finally, neutral allows forward movement and team implementation of a decision when a portion of the team is engaged and even excited about a decision and when this portion of the team is willing to carry the decision implementation through to completion.

ChoiceMark Practices

With this information about the neutral stage of consensus in hand, you are ready to practice recognizing ChoiceMark decision points and selecting language that you can use to move decision discussions forward to an actual decision. These practices are designed for you to build your skills and confidence as a decision maker, as a team leader, and as a team member working with yourself or others when neutral is the mindset for decision making. Read through each scenario. Watch for decision point language and signals. Respond to the questions at the end of each scenario. Also identify which of the four scenarios are similar to situations you experience at work. Then consider how you can now go back and handle your own decision situations with greater effectiveness.

Scenario 1—Recognizing Neutral in Action

The Alpharet purchasing department meeting is under way again. However, this meeting requires new decisions to be made. As you know, every Thursday morning, the Alpharet Company purchasing department holds a staff meeting. Cedric Fredricksen is the meeting leader and is also the director for the purchasing department. Cedric has called an impromptu meeting of his team. The attendees at the meeting include: Joe Anderson, purchasing specialist; Janet Hernandez, purchasing specialist; Fred Alverez, RFP issuing agent; Vic Toney, vendor relations specialist; and Cynthia Thorngaard, quality control specialist. The impromptu meeting is just beginning. How can Cedric gain control of the meeting? His team members are frustrated about having been pulled away from their desks and their existing work.

Cedric: I know, you are all busy, but we have an urgent request to solve a vendor problem yet this afternoon.

Vic: What are you talking about? Why wasn't I called first?

Janet: What happened?

Cynthia: What do we need to do?

Joe: Do we all need to be here?

Cedric: Yes, I need you all here to help solve the problem. This is about our biggest vendor, X Corp. They filed bankruptcy just an hour ago. Legal called me and said they hoped we have a back-up vendor already lined up.

Vic: No way. How could this have happened? We just received a big order from them yesterday.

Cynthia: How long will that shipment last?

Joe: I'll go pull the inventory counts and come back.

Janet: What else do we need to research while Joe gets that information?

Cedric: What other vendors can fill these same orders? Do we have anyone as a backup?

Fred: I'll go pull the file for who submitted the last time we went out for bid on this. It is a few years old but I guess it gives us a starting place.

Cedric: Okay, let's meet back here in ten minutes with all the information each of you can gather to help me get back to legal with our plan of action in the next forty-five minutes.

Questions

1. Who is operating at neutral? How can you tell?

2. If you were Cedric what would you do and say when you lead the next portion of the meeting that starts in ten minutes?

3. How can Vic get to neutral in order to help solve the problem at hand?

Potential Answers

1. Janet and Cynthia are operating at neutral. Right at the start of the impromptu meeting both Janet and Cynthia are asking for information. Cynthia even moves right into problem solving without pointing fingers and without yet committing herself to action.

2. As the meeting starts back in ten minutes, Cedric's goal is to keep Janet and Cynthia in neutral, to move Joe from anti-survival (having hinted that he doesn't even want to be in the meeting) to neutral and a mindset for problem-solving, and to move Vic out of boxed-in and into neutral so that he too can join the problem-solving process. Cedric can start the next portion of the meeting with such neutralizing and direction-giving language as "I know this caught all of us by surprise. I sure wasn't expecting this upset in our purchasing flows. Thanks for collecting the information you've brought back. Now we've got several scenarios to play with from here. First, the bankruptcy prevents them from recovering and so we have to have an alternate supplier permanently. Another scenario might be that they recover from the bankruptcy and we can keep using their parts well into the future. What other scenarios might we be working with?"

3. Vic, as vendor relations specialist, is in shock and feeling like he should have seen this coming. Vic may be able to recognize his boxed-in outlook and refocus his energies into a neutral mindset. However, if he's not able to refocus, one of his team-mates can help by offering: "Vic, hey, this has nothing to do with you. You do a good job for us. Sometimes things just get away and are way beyond our control. We need you on this. We need your knowledge of the company and the players so we can figure out what the bankruptcy will do to them and to us. And we need your ability to build relationships quickly with other vendors as our competitors may already have them locked up. What do you say, can you roll with this and help us build a plan for Cedric to take back to legal?"

Scenario 2—Shifting Neutral into Discussing and Making a Decision

A person in neutral can become so uninvolved in discussions that their needed and relevant expertise is not heard. Determine what you'd do to enlarge the following conversation and ask for input from the team members in neutral before moving to a decision.

Meeting Leader Joshua: Our goal today is to give the marketing team feedback on the list of names they've generated for our new gyroscope product. They've done the market and consumer research and want our input to be sure the product isn't misrepresented.

Susannah: I have an engineering degree and I really don't have any input on this.

Trevor: I'm glad they are finally involving us in the naming of a product. A few product names back almost created a lawsuit over misrepresentation.

Martin with impatience: Well, what are their suggestions?

Noah with hesitance: Yeah, what are we suppose to react to?

Jacob: I'm curious but not committed so tell us what the list includes.

Cyrus: I'm with Trevor. This is a move in the right direction. We need to be included in every product naming.

Questions

1. Which team members are in neutral?

2. If you were leading this meeting, what would you do and say now?

3. If you were Cyrus, what would you do and say to move your team members out of neutral and into decision making?

Potential Answers

1. Jacob, Martin and Noah are in neutral. With Martin and Noah, you can tell because they are open to hearing the product names but have a guarded tone of voice

when they ask for the list. Jacob uses his words to express that he's in neutral "curious but not committed."

2. Joshua as meeting leader can capitalize on the neutral and engaged enthusiasm of participants and invite discussion. "Okay, I'll share the three names. What we are looking for is our number one choice from their list. Then we need to provide reasons why this is our choice. Here are the names..."

3. Cyrus is already in engaged enthusiasm, so he will encourage fellow participants from this mindset. Cyrus could use a conversational approach such as: "I know you guys are not inclined to weigh in on this. It really is an opportunity to build our credibility with marketing. Let's really give Joshua good information to take back to them. Jacob, you have been on more product development teams than any of us. What do you think?"

Scenario 3—Gaining Implementation Commitment from People in Neutral

As you read about earlier in this chapter, when someone leaves a meeting in neutral, any follow up actions or assignments are unlikely to happen at best. In this situation, what will you do to ensure that the person in neutral commits to at least one action item?

Brent: Okay, can we make a decision already?

Jill: I'm ready. And, I'll volunteer to take the market research for the Southeastern part of the United States.

Brent: Good idea. I'll work on the European Union countries research.

Meeting Leader Susan: Great. Thanks for jumping in.

Philip: What's left?

Alain: All the other regions are left. I'll take everything West of the Mississippi.

Philip: Okay. Now what's left?

Jill: Actually, I'll take The whole Eastern seaboard. I've got some ideas on how to tackle this.

Brent: I think we're covered.

Susan: Actually, we still have the Central U.S. to cover as well as Canada. So,...

Questions

1. Which team member is in neutral?

2. As meeting leader, what could you say to get each team member to commit to some level of implementation?

3. How can Brent support Philip's decision to commit to action?

Potential Answers

1. Philip. He asks a few questions hinting that he might help but he never commits to action and doesn't volunteer to take a region, even though he knows all of the regions the company covers.

2. Susan can continue with "So, we're mostly covered. Thanks for jumping in to take the regions you prefer. Philip, which region do you want? Canada or the Central U.S.?" Given his neutrality, asking Philip to take on two regions is likely unrealistic. Some negotiations in the size of research tasks taken on may be necessary. However, when the goal is to get every team member, including those who are in a neutral mindset to participate, realistic workloads need to be assigned.

3. From the start, Brent was committed to action. With the ChoiceMarks knowledge, Brent can recognize that all team members are engaged with the exception of Philip. Brent can then support Susan's need for each team member to commit to action either before or after she speaks. He can suggest "Philip, you know more about Canadian markets than the rest of us. Why don't you take it?" Or, Brent could offer "Philip, if you take both regions, I can get with you to compare what we find and bring it back to the discussion."

Scenario 4—Determining Whether to Stay in Consensus Mode or Shift to Command and Control with People in Neutral

Sometimes people in neutral seem to leave the room, even though they are still sitting in the discussion circle. When a decision is needed in a meeting where the whole team has moved to neutral, it can become time to shift to a command decision and recommend implementation. How can this nearly neutral team meeting moment be moved to decision?

Kaye: I don't have much input. I wasn't involved in the tests or reviews. So, whatever you all decide is the best answer, I'll go along with.

Abby: I think we're good. We can probably move ahead.

Emil: I'm telling you all, our test results don't support this decision.

Andy: How can you say that? One test, with two faulty inputs ended up in a failure to pass.

Ken: I'll support whatever decision you all make. I'm not in this fight.

Emil: I still don't think that this is the right direction. Our structural tests show there is a fault that will cause a fracture.

Abby: We have to make a decision. Today is our timeframe. Risk Management wants the report by 9:00 a.m. on Thursday.

Amir: Is anyone going to make a decision?

Questions

1. Which team members are in neutral? How will they likely respond to a shift to command-and-control decision making?

2. As the meeting leader of this chaotic meeting, how will you step in and move the team to a decision?

3. Would a minority report be useful to this team? How would a minority report benefit them?

Potential Answers

1. Kaye and Ken are in neutral. In this meeting, they have indicated that they'll go along with whatever decision is made. So it is unlikely that they will have any reaction to a shift to command and control.

2. During the meeting moment given, the meeting leader has not commented. Given the call for someone to make a decision, the timing is perfect for the meeting leader to step in. "Abby is correct, today is the timeframe for making this decision. Given what you all have presented, I'm recommending that we approve the test conclusions. However, Emil, I'm also expecting you to prepare a minority report so that your concerns can be documented. On this project, Risk Management has final review and approval so you can rest assured that by producing a minority report your concerns will be seen." Making a statement about what is expected of the group and following it with the expectation for Emil of the preparation of a minority report makes clear that Risk Management is going to receive a go-ahead recommendation along with Emil's concerns.

3. Yes a minority report will be useful. As seen in the potential response to question two, suggesting a minority report be written gives the team direction and a decision from the meeting leader. A minority report is also beneficial to the team because having one will reflect all of the opinions of team members when the presentation is made to Risk Management.

No Decision—No Action

When a team stays in neutral and fails to make a clear decision, no new action and no changed actions result. If things are working well enough as they are, a no-decision discussion result may be harmless to the organization. However, if things are not going well at the time of the decision discussion, failure to reach a decision may very well harm the organization and the people working for it. You've probably heard the saying "not making a decision is a decision." What this really means is that not making a decision to change things or to take a new course is in fact a decision to leave things as they currently exist. Whatever your or your team's results from a neutral position, when making decisions be sure to consider what help or harm will come to the organization. For example, indecision can be a wrong decision when people's health or well-being will be negatively affected as a result of the indecision.

Indecision can also be wrong when a supply chain is at risk of being lost and the loss can cause a plant shutdown. In other words, whenever harm comes to people, a process or system, or to an overall situation, indecision is a wrong or bad decision.

Conversely, indecision can be okay or even good when more information is genuinely needed before a decision can be made. When information is missing, data appears inaccurate, budget details are incomplete, or timelines are uncertain, collecting the needed information before making a decision is reasonable. As long as immediate indecision leads to a short-term assignment to collect and research relevant information and ultimately leads to a final decision to go ahead or not, it can be okay to delay a decision. Indecision can sometimes work out well when new information is becoming available in the midst of the immediate decision discussion. The newly available information may change the entire discussion as well as the resulting decision. Clearly, discernment comes into play when determining whether indecision is good or bad, helpful or harmful to the situation at hand.

Chapter Summary

From a neutral point of view, there are strengths and limitations of living in this mindset and stage of ChoiceMark consensus. With a neutral mindset, I can help move a discussion forward, or let indecision stall the discussion forever. When other mindsets are unable to listen effectively, moving to neutral is a net-benefit to a group because listening for multiple points of view can occur. That's it: I'll move to neutral when fitting and move out of neutral when a clear decision is needed.

CHAPTER 7

Moving Out of Being Boxed-in

Why Move Out?

For decades we've heard about boxed-in thinking and group-think that prevents creative problem solving. In fact, some group-think scenarios have been blamed for business failures and even deaths. The 1986 Challenger Shuttle explosion that killed seven astronauts, including the first teacher in space, is often blamed on a group-think scenario regarding o-ring seals that had prevented best-possible decision making. In this chapter you'll discover how to recognize boxed-in thinking, its benefits and limitations. You'll also learn to ask the questions needed to determine whether individuals and groups can move forward with a decision—whether it is a go or no-go decision.

If you discovered in Chapter 2 that your primary approach to thinking about consensus is boxed-in thinking, your strength is recognizing similar past work efforts on achieving objectives, whether they worked or not. Knowing the history of things can help with current problem solving. Being stuck in past scenarios or in a limited scope of thinking hinders the ability to hear other points of view and to contribute to best-possible decision making. Other people perceive your boxed-in thinking as a limitation because it dampens their enthusiasm, and appears to stand in the way of making an affirmative decision. To increase your problem solving and decision making effectiveness, move out of your boxed-in thinking. Repeating that something won't work doesn't help others understand why it won't work. You can choose to move to anti-survival or to neutral, but at least move. Move to anti-survival when your concerns are not being heard and you realize that being more articulate about your concerns is necessary. Choose to move to neutral to start asking questions of others to learn whether there are workable options that you haven't considered.

When Individuals Reach Boxed-in

Individuals reach boxed-in thinking because of life experiences that have narrowed a person's visions, because of finding a preference for a narrowed field of options, and even because of repeatedly hearing others say "think outside of your box more often." Repeatedly being asked or told to think outside of a comfort zone does not prompt stretched thinking. In fact, it tends to encourage staying in the safety zone of predictable thinking. Inviting someone living in a boxed-in mode to expand or enlarge their views and potential options for considerations can be challenging, yet the reward is better decision making that is based on more relevant information that would have been available had the team not heard from the boxed-in thinker.

When presenting information that challenges people to see other points of view than their boxed-in driven thinking, be prepared for everyone's frustration factor to rise. Here's why. People tired of hearing "it won't work" have a hard time listening to the valuable messages and ideas that can come along to support why something won't work. And people tired of trying to explain why something won't work can feel so unheard that they give up trying to understand others and trying to be understood themselves. Here's a key point: people in every stage of ChoiceMark consensus have a valuable input on the final decision, how it gets made, and what the final decision result actually is. Unless purposefully asked to present and defend a boxed-in set of positions, staying in boxed-in typically prevents a team from making best-possible decisions.

Groups Don't Need to Reach Boxed-in to Make Decisions

To reach best-possible decisions, groups need all consensus stages of thinking. In fact when a group or team reaches an entirely boxed-in position, one of two results occur. One result is that the team reaches a "don't-do-it" decision. The second is that the team will likely reach the conclusion that, "If you do proceed with this, there is only one way to do it." Typically, getting everyone on a team to boxed-in does not help the team to reach a decision. Rather, it creates a festival of ideas for why something won't and can't work. Focus the team on problem solving the current problem. Focus the boxed-in thinkers on, "What needs to be different this time for things to work?" or on, "What would you change to make the proposed idea work?"

Discussion tools, problem-solving processes, and decision tools are not meant to box people in but rather to expand boundaries of thought and to enlarge discussions. Revisiting the comments General Jim Brooks made during our interview (see Chapter 2 for the beginning of his comments), here is one approach to problem solving. Says General Brooks:

The military has a "standard system" of problem solving but most managers tailor their own mechanism. All require strong communication skills. The system I use includes:

1. Identifying the problem or challenge up front. Sometimes this is the hardest part.

2. Gather appropriate staff, define the problem or challenge. Appoint a coordinator.

3. Define what is required of us. Also, define any limitations or places not to go or approaches not to take.

4. Offer initial guidance to include possible solutions and pitfalls.

5. Staff does research, develops options with advantages and disadvantages for each.

6. Assemble the group for decision briefing, recommendations, and discussion.

7. Make the decision.

Problem solving steps 3, 4, and 5 above can benefit from boxed-in thinking because of the need for uncovering limitations, possible pitfalls, and disadvantages. So, said again differently, the key to making best-possible decisions is to draw on the strengths of each ChoiceMark consensus stage. Gathering the reasons something might not work is just as important as hearing how enthusiastic people are to make something work. Uncovering how a decision might hurt people, the team, or the organization is just as important as discovering the pure passion driving people to move an affirmative decision forward for implementation. While consensus-driven decisions take longer to make than command-and-control decisions, the information gathered during the consensus discussions usually uncovers valuable information that contributes to making a best-possible decision that can lead to successful implementation.

Questions to Ask When You Are in Boxed-in

Being boxed-in tends to limit your willingness and ability to listen to other points of view. As a result, others tend to tune you out too. To increase your effectiveness, focus on becoming more open-minded and more articulate about your position and concerns. Use phrases and questions such as the following to expand your viewpoint. Also, use a tone of voice that expresses genuine interest in hearing the responses, or the whole discussion will turn into an exercise in frustration.

- What experiences have you had that suggest this will work?
- What are you seeing that I'm not?
- When could this work?
- How can the approach you all are discussing really work?

- Where has this approach worked?
- What timetables for implementation do you envision? Are they realistic?
- Who has been successful with this approach? Is there an example company we can study?
- Are you willing to hear out my concerns?
- May I please share my experiences as to why this won't work as planned?

Questions to Ask When Others Are in Boxed-in

Recognize that a boxed-in thinker is in a comfort zone that is familiar and appears to work or the person wouldn't want to stay in it. To enlarge a boxed-in thinker's perspective, or to tap a boxed-in thinker's expertise, ask such questions as

- What can you tell us about what went wrong last time?
- What needs to change to make it work this time?
- What modifications might make this work?
- Where did things break down last time?
- What lessons were learned last time that we can use to not make the same mistakes?
- Who else experienced these challenges? Shall we get them to share their expertise too?
- What expertise will prevent us from going down the same path that failed last time?
- Where can we find the details?
- What has changed in the marketplace since this was last tried?
- How have our systems and technologies changed internally since this was last tried?

Just Because Someone Reached Boxed-in, Don't Expect Things Not to Get Done

Typically a boxed-in thinker is against what a team decides, is unlikely to commit to implementation, and is likely to stand in the way of what the team wants to do. However, when a boxed-in thinker is more committed to a cause or project than the desire to stand in the way of achievement, then commitment to implementation can occur. Inviting boxed-in thinkers to participate in decision implementation usually evokes a response of "no" or "no thank you." There are times, however, when boxed-in thinkers really want to participate in implementation, despite their apparent disinterest and willingness to undermine implementation. Keep the invitation to participate clear and succinct: "What part of implementation would you like to handle?" Be sure to take every opportunity to invite people at all stages of the ChoiceMarks consensus continuum to participate in implementation.

Getting Someone in Boxed-in to Shift Mindsets

While boxed-in thinking can seem like a detriment to decision making, it can actually be a more open-minded position than anti-survival. So, when someone is in anti-survival your best hope for getting the person to not stand in the way of decision implementation may be to get to boxed-in. The anti-survival stage of Choice-Mark consensus actively suggests a "don't-do-it" position. A boxed-in thinker offers reasons why something won't work. So getting someone out of the anti-survival stage and into talking about the multitude of reasons something won't work can enlarge the discussion. Conversely, getting someone who is in boxed-in thinking to move to anti-survival thinking can prompt discussion of the real and perceived potential harms that should lead to a "no-go" decision, thus helping the team to make a better decision.

In Chapter 6 you read about how the ChoiceMark continuum corresponds to the verdicts a jury must reach. Yet another way to describe the ChoiceMark continuum of consensus is in terms of day-to-day for or against decision making. Someone in anti-survival is against making a positive decision, doesn't want things to change, and may in fact fight the decision, stand in the way of the decision, and undermine or even sabotage the decision implementation. Someone in boxed-in may be against a positive decision, work actively against the decision, and may or may not stand in the way of the final decision and its implementation. Someone in neutral is not fighting for or against the decision and once the decision is made, may or may not work for a successful implementation of the decision. Next up, engaged enthusiasm is in favor of the decision being made in the affirmative. Someone in engaged enthusiasm will work to get others to make an affirmative decision and to help with its implementation. Finally, someone in extreme excitement is very in favor of making a positive decision, wants things to change, and will do a great deal to make sure the decision gets made in the affirmative and is successfully implemented. By recognizing the continuum of thought associated with the ChoiceMarks, you can help all five of the consensus stage thinkers to shift or enlarge their points of view and their willingness to make decisions.

Back to boxed-in thinking. Someone in boxed-in thinking can benefit from a shift to anti-survival thinking in order to commit to a "don't-do-it" position. Separately, when at the boxed-in stage, shifting to neutral can be useful also. Moving to a neutral mindset can enlarge the decision discussion and solution finding. A shift to neutral can also help prevent a boxed-in thinker from working against a decision and its implementation. Once a shift to neutral occurs, sometimes a previously boxed-in thinker will even shift to engaged enthusiasm and work actively to get the decision implementation to happen successfully.

Boxed-in Thinking Can Be a Good Thing

Yes, boxed-in thinking can be a good thing. When barriers and potential problems need to be uncovered before a decision is made, boxed-in thinking can help. When past problems have gone unsolved, a boxed-in thinker usually knows about them and can share that the problems are still occurring. Boxed-in thinking is helpful also when potential implementation breakdowns need to be identified as a part of the decision discussion. When decisions are made too quickly or such that all relevant points of view are not taken into consideration, missteps, disaster, and even death can follow. Boxed-in thinking can contribute to slowing the timing of a decision that is for the good consideration of potential problems. Boxed-in thinking can also contribute to uncovering relevant past problems that can be avoided this time. Invite boxed-in thinkers to contribute to every decision discussion to ensure that best-possible decisions are reached.

ChoiceMark Practices

With a new understanding of boxed-in thinkers, you can continue practicing to recognize ChoiceMark decision points and select language that you can use to move decision discussions forward to an actual decision. Practice identifying discussion decision points and crafting language that would work in the scenario to move the team toward a decision. These additional practices are still designed for you to build your skills and confidence as an individual decision maker, as a team leader, and as a team member. Read through each scenario. Watch for decision point language and signals. Respond to the questions at the end of each scenario. Also identify which of the four scenarios are similar to situations you've experienced and consider how you can now go back and handle your own decision situations more effectively.

Scenario 1—Recognizing Boxed-in in Action

Sometimes boxed-in is present and clearly visible in a meeting. Other times it is subtle and requires an invitation to contribute insights to the team discussion. As you know, every Thursday morning, the Alpharet Company purchasing department holds a staff meeting for the purpose of identifying new products needed by the company, updating request for proposal statuses, and updating back-ordered products that may require finding new suppliers. Cedric Fredricksen is the meeting leader and is also the director for the purchasing department. The attendees at the meeting include Joe Anderson, purchasing specialist; Janet Hernandez, purchasing specialist; Cynthia Thorngaard, quality control specialist; and Vic Toney, vendor relations specialist. Absent from the meeting is Fred Alverez, RFP issuing agent. Today's staff meeting is running longer than usual because of another big decision, this time about forecasting annual price increases from vendors. And again, nearly everyone is frustrated.

Cynthia: Cedric, did you say we have to make a decision today on the upcoming year's projected price increases for everything the company buys?

Cedric: Yes. We've had three months to work with vendors, ask them what they are projecting, look for new vendors where needed and pencil our projections.

Janet: I still need more time. Not everyone responded to my calls for information.

Vic: I've got some already announced price-sheets for several vendors. I can give them to whoever is doing our master calculation spreadsheet.

Cynthia: That will help but I agree with Janet in that we really don't have enough information to finalize projections today.

Joe: My vendor list of price increases is done. Cedric I can give it to you.

Vic: Janet, who else do you need information from? I can help track some details down.

Janet: I'll go to my desk and get the list.

Cedric: Okay. Before you leave. . .

Questions

1. Who is at boxed-in? How can you tell?

2. If you were Cedric what would you do and say to get the participants to move toward the projections decision?

3. If you were Vic, what would you do and say to get your co-workers to reach agreement on what actions to take?

4. If you were Janet, what would you do and say to get a decision made during this meeting?

Potential Answers

1. Janet and Cynthia appear to be boxed-in because of not having all the information they feel is needed to make the final projection of price increases.

2. As meeting leader, Cedric is now up against a deadline for decision making because his team members aren't ready to commit to projections in today's meeting. As a result, he may choose to use a more command-and-control approach to moving the team forward: "Vic, thanks for offering to get the needed price sheets. Joe, thanks for finishing your vendor projections. Where else can you help run numbers for us?" (Wait for his response before continuing.) "Janet and Cynthia let's get together this afternoon at 2:00 so we can confirm what information you need to have before we finalize the projections at our meeting next week. And I'll get with Fred to see where his numbers are."

3. Vic has offered already to help track down information from an engaged enthusiasm point of view. He could additionally offer, "Once I get the needed price sheets for next year, then what do you want me to do so we can make our projections at our next meeting?"

4. Janet is one of the people feeling boxed-in by the limited amount of information that she has at hand. Her most likely approach would be to get the team to delay its final decision. Janet might suggest, "Cedric, can we have one more week to work out the projections?" or she might ask, "Who can help me run the calculations once I have the pricing?"

Scenario 2—Shifting Boxed-in into Recognizing Other Points of View

A person in boxed-in can get so focused on the points of view that indicate how something won't work that others feel their positive can-do-it ideas are not being listened to. Determine what you'd do to enlarge the following frustrated and lacking-in-focus conversation before moving to a decision.

Pam: All you ever focus on is what won't work.

Peter: We'll I've experienced a lot and know what won't work.

Thomas: Okay you two, enough. Every other meeting you get into this.

Tiffany: Stephanie, didn't you say our goal is to focus on finding a solution to the customer's complaint that our machines are breaking down on their floor every fifteen days?

Stephanie: Yes.

Star: Well, of the ideas we've kicked around so far, I don't think any of them will work.

Questions

1. Who is in boxed-in thinking mode?

2. If you are the meeting leader, what will you do or say now to encourage more idea generation?

3. What can Star and Peter do or say to move themselves out of boxed-in and into helping make a decision?

Potential Answers

1. Star and Peter are in boxed-in thinking. They are both focused on what won't work.

2. The team has not yet heard why the possible solutions discussed "won't work." As meeting leader, work to discover why Star and Peter are putting up barriers to the ideas already discussed. "Star, pick one solution and tell us what about it won't work please." (Wait for her responses.) Separately, ask Peter, "You're right. You have more experience than any of us with this machine of ours. What do you think can work to fix the problem the customer is having?" (Wait for his response.) Whatever spoken words the meeting leader uses an inviting tone when asking each question followed by a long silence is critical to getting input from people who are boxed-in.

3. Boxed-in thinkers can expand their own thinking by asking themselves, "What do I see that can be changed to make this solution work?"

Scenario 3—Gaining Implementation Commitment from Boxed-in Thinkers

Someone set in boxed-in thinking may not stand in the way of making the decision because of being resigned to the fact that sometimes a lack of agreement with a decision doesn't prevent it from getting made. Just because someone has expressed boxed-in thinking doesn't mean a lack of participation in implementation will result. Getting a boxed-in thinker to participate in implementation is more challenging than getting a neutral person to participate in decision implementation. Let's revisit a meeting from Chapter 4. What can this meeting leader do to gain implementation commitment from the team members in boxed-in?

Meeting Leader: Okay. We've generated a lot of ideas today. And we just agreed to build an implementation plan for our decision to add connecting cable production to our existing hardware product line.

Joyce: Right. I'm in project overload right now. Can you get this done without me?

Jim: I guess I can help out. What needs to be done?

Jaclyn: We've been waiting for this decision a long time. I'm surprised you all aren't more excited about finally moving forward. I'm in. I'll help get this done. In fact, I'll check in with accounting to confirm what dollar amount is available for implementation. And, I'll check with training to see when we can roll out the new machine-operator training. Then, I can talk to production to see what their needs are for adding connecting cable manufacturing onto the floor.

Jacque: We better get with production. This plan will change a lot of their floor-space, inventory, and staffing needs. I'm not convinced we should be moving ahead with this without talking to them. Production needs to have input and a final say on this. Let's slow down with our final decision.

JoAnn: I'm with Jacque. We've run into problems before with such fast-paced changes and we need to get the right people into the discussion.

Jake: Customers have spoken. We need to add this to our product offerings or we risk losing even our existing sales. We've made the decision to move forward. Let's do that and we can always regroup after we've gotten the next round of planning for implementation done.

Questions

1. Which team member(s) are boxed-in?

2. As meeting leader in the above meeting, what will you do or say to ensure that successful implementation happens with the team members in boxed-in thinking mode?

Potential Answers

1. Jacque and JoAnn are in boxed-in thinking mode. And in this case, the rest of the team needs to listen to their points of view to make sure that the decision's

implementation can happen successfully. The meeting leader can serve the group best by getting more details from Jacque and JoAnn: "Okay, what else do we need to be considering before we move forward?"

2. Because input really is needed from the production team as Jacque suggested, the meeting leader's challenge is balancing the drive to keep moving forward that half of the team has with the relevant concerns JoAnn and Jacque have expressed. No fixed deadline has been given in the discussion so delaying a decision to ensure relevant inputs are considered is an option. You could say, "You all have expressed both great ideas for moving ahead and some real and relevant concerns about moving ahead. Because production will be greatly affected by our decision, we really do need their input. Jacque and JoAnn, will you get with me and the product team this afternoon? And then we'll all meet together again as a team tomorrow afternoon to finalize our decision with the production team's input." Then, when it comes time for action, to involve everyone in the implementation you can say, "We spent the necessary time to make a best-possible decision and involve each of the affected departments—thanks. Now we're ready to move ahead. What element of implementation will each of you take part in?" Now, wait for each person to volunteer. If some team members don't volunteer, you may consider suggesting or assigning their responsibilities for action.

Scenario 4—Determining Whether to Stay in Consensus Mode or Shift to Command and Control with People in Boxed-in

Sometimes people in boxed-in work so hard to get others to join them in their position that the ideas under consideration can't possibly work that time runs short for making a decision. When a decision is needed in the same meeting that a stalled discussion is occurring, it becomes time to shift to a command decision and recommend implementation. How can this boxed-in meeting moment be moved to decision?

Meeting Leader Donna: We need a decision to be made in this meeting. We all knew today was decision-time.

Doug: Yes, but the data has changed in just the last three days. If we don't take it into account, I think we'll make the wrong decision.

Denise: True, the data changed for one small segment of our user group. Can't we go ahead with the largest portion of customer concerns and base our decision on that?

Doug: I don't think so.

Duncan: Denise might have a point. What if we separate our users into subgroups and determine how large each group is before we decide what to move forward?

Doug: I think it affects every group.

Donavan: How do you know?

Delores: Yes. What information can you share with us that will persuade us to not make any changes at all?

Questions

1. Which team members are thinking from boxed-in positions?

2. As the meeting leader of this going-nowhere meeting, how will you step in and move the team to a decision?

3. If you are Donavan, how could you help the meeting leader move the talk to a decision?

Potential Answers

1. Doug is thinking from a boxed-in, won't-work position. His statements about not going ahead and not having accurate data are communicating his position.

2. Donna can move the meeting forward by giving directions regarding what must be considered now in order to get a decision for action made today. She might ask the following series of questions: "What harm will come from making the change? What could be modified to allow this to work? Is there any component of the project you'd be willing to work on Doug?"

3. Donavan's ChoiceMark mindset is not clear here. However, his willingness to ask questions makes it reasonable to think he would make a statement or ask questions from any of the ChoiceMark mindsets to help move the meeting forward.

With four of the five ChoiceMark practices completed, your increasing skill in recognizing mindsets, hearing decision points, and asking questions can improve everyday decision making.

Chapter Summary

I recognize my strength is seeing why things won't work. Now, I'll focus on improving my ability to articulate both why things won't work and what can be changed to allow solutions to work. Unless I'm specifically asked to use my strengths as a boxed-in thinker, I'll work to improve my listening skills and be more open minded about other points of view. Enough already; no need to belabor the point!

CHAPTER 8

Listening to Anti-Survival for Good Decision Making

Killing an Idea Is Sometimes Best

Sometimes nay-sayer, kill-the-idea, or anti-survival thinking is on track. Here's why. Problem solutions that put people or organizations at risk or in harm's way often should be avoided, passed on, or voted down. Decisions that create threats to safety, to continuous operation, or to the environment are also worth being opposed. Anti-survival thinking recognizes problems, missing links, and threats quickly. The focus of anti-survival thinking is on identifying elements that can cause death or serious harm to an individual or to an organization. The value of anti-survival thinking is that when there are problems, potential breakdowns, or possible threats that can result from a decision, anti-survival thinkers can spot and describe them.

The phrase anti-survival means being in opposition to the ideas or the decision at hand because of severe concerns about safety and about the actual survival capacity of individuals and organizations if the decision is made. Said another way, the decision under consideration is perceived as preventing the reasonable survival of individuals or the organization and so in the objection to the decision the anti-survival thinker is fighting for the survival of individuals and organizations. Said even more simply, anti-survival thinking says, "Don't make this decision this way."

When Individuals Reach Anti-Survival

Individuals reach anti-survival when past experience shows there is a threat, when the currently offered solution has clear flaws, or when a gut instinct shouts "danger." Individuals in anti-survival will work against the decision at hand because of their deep concerns and their desire to see a best-possible decision made from their point of view. Anti-survival thinking can surface also when individuals feel a personal threat to their well-being, to the security of their jobs, or to the well-being of people they care about. When individuals reach anti-survival, it is as powerful a state of being as being in extreme excitement. Both stages of ChoiceMarks consensus have equal parts passion and commitment to seeing their preferences, points of view, and ideas implemented. Individuals in an anti-survival mindset are often so focused on their concerns that an inability or unwillingness to listen to others seems to take hold.

When individuals reach anti-survival there are times that redirecting or expanding their focus can be difficult because of the already high level of commitment to concerns that appear to cause harm to people, property, or the environment. In order to get other ideas and input heard by people in anti-survival, present information in ways that will validate the concerns and at the same time offer opposing points of view. Describe potential solutions and invite an enlarged consideration of what action is best to agree to move forward upon. When presenting information that challenges the positions of people in anti-survival, be prepared for push-back, upset, and even anger. Stay your course and continue to state your optimism, realistic solutions, and overall case because decision making does not require everyone to be at the same ChoiceMark stage for a decision to be made.

Groups Don't Need to Reach Anti-Survival to Make Decisions

Groups need to hear from the anti-survival point of view in order to consider the affects of decisions accurately. However, getting everyone on a team to anti-survival is unproductive because discussing only the "don't-do-it" concerns surrounding a decision prevents the possibility thinking of engaged enthusiasm and extreme excitement from being heard and potentially offering viable solutions. Having at least one member on the team thinking through a decision from the anti-survival mindset is beneficial because downsides, potential pitfalls, and outright dangers can be identified during rather than after the decision-making process.

In Chapter 7, the point was made that boxed-in thinkers can benefit by shifting to neutral or to anti-survival in order to contribute to making a final decision. Ultimately, teams and decision making units are best served when all five of the Choice-Marks stages of consensus are represented mindsets and when at least the meeting leader has a mastery of both command-and-control as well as consensus-driven decision making. When a team has only the polarized anti-survival and extreme excitement mindsets represented, battles for the final decision break out because the middle ground for expanding the conversation to reach a best-possible decision is not represented. When a team has only boxed-in and anti-survival thinking going on, the decision is doomed from the start, which may or may not be a bad thing because some decision directions really are not worth pursuing.

Questions to Ask When You Are in Anti-Survival

Reaching an anti-survival mindset means you have great concern for the safety of people, property, systems, and the environment. Your heightened concerns can make it difficult for you to listen to other points of view. While still holding your position so that you can share your concerns with the team, focus on also listening to other points of view, mindsets, and potential solutions that would cause less concern and even be viable solutions. When you are in anti-survival, to enlarge your sense of what might be possible, ask others such questions as the following:

- Have you seen this work? Where?
- What is driving this exact decision?
- When does the decision absolutely have to be made? Maybe we can talk through more options.
- How long can we delay the decision so we can gather more information?
- Where can we see that this plan has been safely implemented?
- What safety record can you show me to ease my concerns?
- What are two alternate approaches to solving this problem that are less likely to cause harm?
- How can we ensure no harm comes from this decision?
- How can we protect our employees?
- How can we protect company property during this decision's implementation?

Questions to Ask When Others Are in Anti-Survival

"This is a bad choice. Someone or something is going to get hurt. We should decide against this." These are the messages someone in anti-survival is communicating to the team. Recognize that the turn-it-down or say-no sentiment comes from concern for the safety and well-being of people and of the organization. To understand the anti-survival point of view and to enlarge the decision discussion, ask such questions or make statements such as the following:

- What harm do you see coming from this approach?
- What methods of prevention can we use to ensure problems do not come up?
- Where can we look for examples of things failing in the way you are predicting?
- What research can be done to overcome the challenges and concerns?
- How can the concerns be overcome?
- When is a system like we are talking about most likely to fail?
- When has an implementation plan like this failed in the past?
- Please tell us what your number one concern is about the direction we are headed because we are ready to move forward.

Just Because Someone Reaches Anti-Survival, Don't Expect Nothing to Get Done

When a whole team reaches anti-survival and or the whole team agrees to be against a decision and its implementation, things don't change. When one or a few team members reach anti-survival and as long as they agree not to block implementation, work can still proceed without them. However, there are times that the anti-survival thinker will participate in implementation, just as there are for boxed-in thinkers. For instance, when the passion for a cause or project is greater than the concerns and/or when concerns can be overcome with adjustments or improved information, then more team members than not are likely to participate in decision implementation. Encourage participation in problem solving by using such phrases as, "You've got a lot of knowledge in this area. What do see as reasonable options for solving this problem?" And to encourage decision-making participation use phrases such as, "You've expressed concerns about the options on the table. What needs to change for there to be a strong solution that we could approve?" Finally, to encourage decision implementation, two approaches may work. First, when someone refuses to participate in implementation, offer, "I understand you are not in support of this decision. The rest of the team is and we need to successfully implement it. So, I need your commitment to not interfere with implementation and a commitment to be available when questions come up because you do have expertise we'll likely need. What do you say? Can you help the team out this way?" Second, when someone has voiced concerns yet hasn't refused to help get things done, consider phrases such as, "Thanks for voicing your concerns. We've built in some safeguards to be sure the project doesn't fall apart as a result of your input. Can we count on your help with implementation? What part would you like to lead or do?"

Recognize Whether People at the Anti-Survival Stage Are Right

Learning to recognize whether people in anti-survival are actually right to challenge the group and to encourage a no-go, don't-do-it decision can save teams from implementation problems as well as the potential of project sabotage. When genuine safety threats exist, anti-survival thinkers are right to challenge the team's thinking and solution choices. The discernment discussions from previous chapters apply here too. Moving everyone to alarm unnecessarily is unproductive. Leaving anti-survival thinkers in anti-survival without addressing their concerns can cause projects to be undermined in the name of protecting everyone. And, learning how to invite anti-survival thinking when barriers and potential problems need to be uncovered before a decision is made can save a work unit from frustrating and even harmful events that could have been planned for or avoided. When the views and concerns of anti-survival thinking are not taken into consideration, problems have the potential of overwhelming agreed-upon solutions. Asking someone to think about what won't work from the boxed-in perspective as well as asking someone with strong anti-survival thinking skills what problems or harm might arise from the solutions under consideration is valuable to the decision-making process.

Invite anti-survival thinkers to share their concerns by using any of the phrases from the *Questions to Ask When Others Are in Anti-Survival* section above. When you can demonstrate that the concerns being expressed are unfounded or can be overcome because new data, systems, or processes are in place that prevent harm from occurring you can often get people to move to neutral. Another time anti-survival thinkers demonstrate a willingness to move to neutral is when a team can demonstrate how the anti-survival concerns can be overcome. The endpoint goal of discussion is best-possible decision making so hearing all points of view and all concerns is critical to achieving that end.

Listen for Hooks and Speak Segues

As you strive to improve your discernment, add ChoiceMarks listening to your communication skill set. Also add the ability to hear conversational hooks and speak conversational segues to keep a decision discussion alive and moving toward a decision. Hooks are key words and phrases that seem important to the speaker or sound important to the listener. Conversation and discussion hooks are also the ideas, concepts, emotions, places, people, and activities that someone else mentions during their comments, questions, information sharing, or storytelling. Listen for the hooks that allow you to create the questions and segues that uncover needed information and allow for enlarged discussions that lead to best-possible decisions. Hook words are important to repeat in the questions you ask and statements you make so that the original speaker and other listeners know your were listening and are being relevant with what you are now contributing to the conversation.

When a decision discussion is just starting, presentations are made, problems are defined, goals are revisited and comments are traded. During the discussion, questions get asked, statements get made in support of and in opposition to ideas. Ideas are also generated for the purpose of solving problems and reaching decisions. In every stage of a decision discussion, conversational hooks can be found that allow an astute listener to offer a conversational segue that enlarges, redirects, or ends a part of the overall decision discussion. Segues are the sentences and questions you can use after finding hook words and phrases. The purpose of a segue is to move a conversation forward in a relevant or a completely different direction. Decision-making discussions demand that the conversation moves forward rather than getting stuck spinning on the same subject. All of the ChoiceMarks sentences and questions presented in Chapters 4 through 8 are examples of segues. Both boxed-in and anti-survival thinkers actively offer this hook: "It won't work." Recognition of this hook allows a segue question to be created to enlarge the conversation and uncover any real barriers to implementation success: "What specifically won't work?"

During every decision discussion, team members are responsible for sharing their experiences, expertise, and ideas. Thinking from a preferred ChoiceMarks stage of consensus as well as being open minded to the input from the other four Choice-Mark stages is also helpful when striving to make best-possible decisions. After listening carefully (see the listening tips in Chapter 4) for hook words, discussion segues can be built. Again, segues are sentences or questions that bridge a current conversation into an enlarged discussion or an entirely new conversation. Conversations can be blame oriented or focus on idea generation. Conversations also can be problem solving or work-assignment giving in nature. In the workplace, the vast majority of conversational discussions lead to (or should) some form of a decision. The end of a decision-making discussion is best handled by summarizing who has agreed to do what by when. This end of discussion summary can become the minutes document which then serves as a project to do list and as a tool for holding individuals and the whole of the team accountable for work completion. Many decision-making and work-accomplishing teams forget this last step of documentation which makes work accomplishment difficult to track and tends to create meeting scenarios in which a team has the same meeting over and over. Repeat meetings without forward progress move team members into anti-survival because they no longer want to waste time in meetings. These go-nowhere meetings also move the team into anti-survival because an overwhelming desire to quit the team and even the company can take over. Again, the key is to focus on the hook words and phrases that hint at what is important. Listen for the hooks, build and offer a segue, and then move the meeting discussion toward a decision.

Practice finding the hooks in the sentences that follow. Look for the hooks that would expand a conversation in directions that may be of interest to the speaker or to the team focused on making a decision.

A. "Over the weekend, I hurt my back while gardening." Which are the "hook" words or phrases?

Answer: In this one sentence there are three potential hooks: weekend activities, hurt back, and gardening. Each hook provides a starting place for expanding a conversation or for ending the discussion. For instance, this segue could end a lengthy discussion that appears to sidetrack the decision discussion: "I'm sorry you hurt your back. I hope you feel better soon. Will you still be able to help get this week's project checklist done?"

B. "We need not fear the expression of ideas—we do need to fear their suppression."
—President Harry S. Truman. Which are the "hook" words or phrases?

Answer: In this quote from President Truman, there are four potential hooks: do not fear, expression of ideas, fear, fear suppression of ideas. As for potential segues, a boxed-in mode segue might be, "Ideas have always been suppressed. Nothing is going to change." And an anti-survival mode segue could be, "I think Truman is right: suppressing the expression of ideas is something to fear because when all ideas are not heard, our decisions are not as strong as they can be. So, I'd like to restate what my concerns are...."

C. "Nice work if you can get it, and you can get it, if you try."—Ira Gershwin. Which are the "hook" words or phrases?

Answer: There are four potential hooks: nice work, work you can get, you can get it, and you can get it if you try.

D. "You can't just sit there and wait for people to give you that golden dream, you've got to get out there and make it happen yourself."—Diana Ross. Which are the "hook" words or phrases?

Answer: There are six potential hooks: can't just sit there, sit there and wait, golden dream, get out there, make it happen, and make it happen yourself. Here are six potential segues, each from a different ChoiceMarks point of view and each of which would move the conversation in a different direction.Extreme excitement segue: "What is the golden dream you're going after?"Engaged enthusiasm segue: "What causes you to feel like you can make things happen yourself?Neutral segue: "I wish dreams would come true while sitting and waiting."Boxed-in segue: "I know we all have to get out there to make things happen but why will this time be different? What will allow us to get anything done?"Anti-survival segue: "I can just sit here. It seems a whole lot safer than going out on a limb that can break."

E. "Wherever you see a successful business, someone once made a courageous decision."—Peter Drucker. Which are the "hook" words or phrases?

Answer: There are five potential hooks that come from the ChoiceMark stages of extreme excitement and engaged enthusiasm: seeing success, successful business, making courageous decisions, courage, and decisions.

F. "Remember that happiness is a way of travel—not a destination."—Roy M. Goodman. Which are the "hook" words or phrases?

Answer: There are four potential hooks: happiness, happiness is a way of travel, travel versus destinations, and happiness is not a destination.

G. From earlier in this chapter, here are some phrases often heard by anti-survival thinkers."This is a bad choice. Someone or something is going to get hurt. We should decide against this." Which are the "hook" words or phrases? And what segues can you build from the hooks?

Answer: There are five hooks: bad choice, someone is going to get hurt, something is going to get hurt, we should decide, and decide against this. Segue options: What makes this a bad choice? Who is likely to get hurt—what job do they do? What is going to get hurt? I agree, let's decide. What specifically should prompt us to decide against this?

Whatever ChoiceMarks consensus stage or degree of command-and-control decision making that is required in a situation, listening for hooks and speaking segues can keep a discussion on track, focused on problem solving, and headed toward reaching a clear decision. Now for the anti-survival practices that will complete the five ChoiceMarks practice sets. With all of the ChoiceMark stages of consensus now in your toolbox, you are ready to finish your practice with recognizing Choice-Mark decision points and selecting language that you can use to move decision discussions forward to an actual decision.

ChoiceMark Practices

As with the past practices, read through each scenario. This time watch for decision point hooks and segues. Respond to the questions at the end of each scenario. And identify which of the four scenarios are similar to situations you've experienced. Then begin planning how you can handle your own daily decision situations with greater effectiveness.

Scenario 1—Recognizing Anti-Survival in Action

Just as with extreme excitement, sometimes anti-survival is loud and visible. Other times it is subtle. In this purchasing department staff meeting, identify the two people who are demonstrating anti-survival. Here's a final Thursday morning, team meeting with the Alpharet Company's purchasing department. Today's focus is on defining the job requirements of a new position that has been funded for the department. Cedric Fredricksen is the meeting leader and is also the director for the purchasing department. The attendees at the meeting include the entire team: Joe Anderson, purchasing specialist; Janet Hernandez, purchasing specialist; Fred Alverez, RFP issuing agent; Vic Toney, vendor relations specialist; and Cynthia Thorngaard, quality control specialist. The staff meeting is once again 35 minutes into its hour-long meeting and discussion has stalled during the definition stage for the new position.

Cedric: I'm sensing a lot of tension around this discussion about job responsibilities. The new position is not going to take away from your responsibilities. We've all complained over the last two years that the demands on our department are unreasonable. Now we get to add a full-time staff person and you all are shying away from it. What's going on?

Janet: We're still in disbelief I think. I for one really can't believe we're finally getting help.

Cedric: We are. The budget commitment is set for a March 1, start date. So let's focus on what work we need to have done and draw up the job requirements so I can submit them to HR for a job description to be created. You all know the HR process is similar to our purchasing process and can take months to complete so that we end up with a new team member.

Fred: Makes sense. Cedric, what information are you really looking for from us?

Cedric: Two things: a list of all the work that we haven't been able to stay on top of and then a list of the skills a person would need to have to get that work done. Then I'll work with HR to figure out what the position title should be.

Vic: As eager as I am for help in our department, I don't think having two vendor relations team members will be appealing to our vendors. I should be the sole contact person.

Cynthia: Well, knowing that we were going to talk about this today, I drafted a list of projects that are undone and skills that I think a new person needs to have to join this team.

Joe: As always, you are organized Cynthia. However, Vic and I have talked about this at length. There's not a good way to dump parts of each of our jobs onto a new person and expect them to be successful. Let's wait until we have enough work for one person to focus on one set of tasks.

Vic: I agree with Joe. I think we should keep going as we are. We work together really well.

Janet: How badly can things turn out? We've been given the budget. Let's get someone in here to help.

Cedric: Okay...

Questions

1. Which two team members are interacting from a position of anti-survival in this meeting?

2. What can Cedric do to keep all of his team members in the discussion?

3. How can Joe and Vic shift their anti-survival mindset to at least neutral?

Potential Answers

1. Joe and Vic are both speaking from an anti-survival mindset. For reasons not fully described yet in this meeting, they both are against the move to hire a new person even though the budget is committed.

2. To keep everyone in the discussion, Cedric can go around the table and suggest the following to each team member:

To Vic: "I hear your concerns. I'm not suggesting a second vendor relations person. Think about what you can use help with behind the scenes, here in the office. Having someone support your work will allow you to focus more energy on your vendor list. Please get a list of in-office jobs you'd like help with to me by tomorrow morning. Then we can get together to refine what you might want in a new person's skill sets."

To Joe: "You're right. A piecemeal job will not be rewarding to the person who takes it. However, having an in-office entry level purchasing specialist who can help us all with things like research, filing, and paper management can make all of our jobs more efficient. Let's focus on what we most need help with that we individually are not getting to. Joe, I really need to know what you'd like support work on. Please give me a list of your top items by tomorrow morning. Then you, Vic, and I can get together to refine the skills it looks like will be needed."

To Cynthia: "Thanks for preparing a list for today. I'll take a look at it and get back to you with any questions I have."

To Janet: "Thanks for being willing to give this situation a try. I'm confident that we'll all be glad to have one more person to help us get work done."

To Fred: "You asked what information I'm looking for. Ultimately we need a list of the skills and knowledge a person will need to work successfully in this department. From your perspective, please draft a list of ten things that you think are needed."

3. Vic and Joe appear to be completely against the hiring of a new person. They may choose to listen to everyone else's point of view in this meeting. Or, it may take a few more discussions with Cedric. In order to invite their open-mindedness or neutral mindsets in this meeting, Cedric can take the approach listed in the answers for number 2 above. Other team members could also invite openness to the new hire idea by using such approaches as the following.

Janet: I wasn't too sure about this hiring idea when we first discussed it either. Now that I've thought about it for a few weeks, I've discovered that there are some parts of my job that are not being done as well as I really want them to be. We can all use some in-office help.

Cynthia: I was in the same spot as Janet. Then, I thought about all the improvements we can make with just one more person. That's when I started drafting the list I just gave Cedric.

Fred: Just think about the vendor bankruptcy scenario we worked through a few months ago. Having one more person to do research for us would have really helped. I think Cedric is right. We need to bring on a new person as soon as the budget is available.

Scenario 2—Shifting Anti-Survival into Recognizing Other Points of View

A person in anti-survival can get so focused on one point of view that others feel they are not being listened to. Determine what you'd do to enlarge the following conversation before moving to a decision. The ConsulArch company is a business services consulting firm. The accounting team has grown frustrated with the sales team for sloppy reports that typically are missing information. Today's meeting focus is on getting more complete and accurate reports from the sales team members. Let's join the meeting.

Meeting Leader and Accounting Manger Frank: We need to identify what information is most often missing from the sales reports and from the reimbursement requests. I have a commitment from the sales manager that he'll work with his team to gain improvements.

Cheryl: It's about time. Sales is notoriously bad about filling in all of the information we need. Then they complain about not getting fully reimbursed for expenses.

Julie: We're lucky to get the information we get now. We've tried for years to get better information and it never seems to work.

Frank: This time is different. We have the executive team's support to make changes because they are not getting accurate and timely sales reports. And they want better reports for their projections.

Julie: I just don't know. I think we'll end up worse off than we are now.

Bryan: This time really sounds different. Frank has said that the sales manager is committed to improvement and that the executive team is backing up the changes too. We need to run with this support.

Julie: Really. I think we should leave well enough alone. When sales people feel the financial pain of their omissions maybe they'll decide to improve their submissions.

Robert: That's a pretty harsh approach...

Questions

1. Who is in anti-survival thinking?

2. What can Frank do to help everyone recognize each others' points of view?

Potential Answers

1. Julie is in anti-survival and against the decision for changed reporting requirements. She repeatedly indicates her position with words such as "it never seems to work;" I think we'll end up worse off;" and "leave well enough alone."

2. Most of Frank's team members seem willing to help make the changes. Yet, those willing to help are having a hard time hearing Julie's real concerns and Julie is having a hard time accepting others' enthusiasm for making the changes. Frank can restate each of the points of view in order to help each team member hear the other. "Julie, I hear that you have reservations about this change working. What specifically looks like it won't work this time?" Frank and the whole team now wait and listen. Then, Frank can restate Julie's expressed concerns before asking others about their positions. "What about the reasons this can work this time? What do you all think we should focus on?"

Scenario 3—Gaining a No-Sabotage Commitment from Anti-Survival Mindsets

Not every team member in each of the ChoiceMarks mindsets will participate in every decision. Discernment includes recognizing who really does need to work on individual projects. And sometimes when a team member is locked in anti-survival mode, unable or unwilling to shift to neutral, the best commitment you can get is one of not sabotaging and not undermining the accomplishment of the team's agreed upon decision. Without this commitment to stand clear and not interfere, the team ends up embarking on a course of action riddled with daily challenges that can prevent successful decision implementation.

Katherine: This simply is not the right course of action.

Meeting Leader Cathy: Katherine, you've said that several times now and yet I haven't heard why you're convinced that it is not right.

Katherine: It's just not.

Bill: Well, who might be hurt if we make this decision?

Katherine: No one person, but the system won't handle the stress this will add.

Bill: Okay. What stresses are we adding that are so great that something will break down?

Katherine: I'll get back to you with the specifics. I've got huge reservations that you all just aren't hearing.

Ed: We're trying but without any specifics, we can't adjust our action plan to address your concerns. I think we need to move ahead.

Cathy: This does require our decision today...

Questions

1. Who is in anti-survival mode and unwilling to shift positions?

2. What would you do as meeting leader to gain commitment for action and for noninterference?

Potential Answers

1. Katherine is in anti-survival mode. The team has asked appropriate Choice-Marks questions and she is still unwilling to shift her position. And yet, she has not articulated clearly where the problems are that she's so concerned about.

2. Cathy can take one of several approaches to help the team move forward to action. While still in the meeting, Cathy can suggest, "Ed is on track. We need to make an implementation decision today and move forward. Can most of us agree to move ahead as proposed?" Then, Cathy waits for verbal or nonverbal team member commitments. When she's heard from the majority of the team, and if the team appears to be in favor of moving ahead Cathy can say, "More than half of us are in agreement to move forward. Ed and Bill, will you co-chair this effort?" Then Cathy can suggest "I'll get with each of you individually to figure out how you want or don't want to participate in implementation. This project doesn't require

everyone's involvement; however, other projects do and will." If the meeting tension is too high for the previous approach, Cathy can immediately move to individual meetings in which she can person by person figure out who is willing to do what. Either way, the best place to seek a no-sabotage commitment is in the individual meetings so that no one is put on the spot in front of other team members. Cathy's next step is to meet with Katherine to learn what her real concerns are and to ask "Katherine, can I count on you to let the team get this done? If they run into challenges, can they come talk with you to get suggestions for overcoming the breakdown?"

Scenario 4—Determining How to Shift to Command and Control with People in Anti-Survival

Sometimes people in anti-survival work so hard to get others to join them in their against-the-decision excitement that time runs short for making a decision. When consensus-reaching discussions have ground to a halt, the need for command and control becomes clear. The ultimate challenge is to shift form consensus to command and control while maintaining every team member's willingness to work with the team. How can this meeting moment be moved to decision?

Robert: There are serious concerns on the table, along with what seem to be legitimate solutions for overcoming the concerns...

Samia: We can make it work. The structural concerns can be overcome.

Mansur: How? Every attempt at this has caused us to lose equipment or worse, deal with worker's compensation issues.

Faye: In fact, two of my field team members were lost. I'm not willing to go down this road again.

Dan: We can't delay any more. We have to make a decision today.

Questions

1. Who is in anti-survival and unwilling to listen to other points of view?

2. What command-and-control sentence or question will you use to get a decision made and post-meeting action to occur?

Potential Answers

1. Mansur and Faye are against the decision and have offered their concerns into the discussion.

2. Any of these command-and-control approaches could work with this team. "We have to make a decision. We can't leave this hanging open. How many of you are in favor of pulling the plug and ending this project?" Or a vote could also be taken in the affirmative: "We have to make a decision today. How many of you are in favor of continuing with the project?" Still another segue approach: "I think the

concerns Faye and Mansur have expressed are serious enough that we should not proceed. Let's close this project down. What do we need to close it down?" Or in the affirmative command form of direction giving: "I think the concerns can be overcome. Our technologies have improved. Let's figure out how we can move ahead safely."

With all five of the ChoiceMark practices completed, your increasing skill in recognizing mindsets, hearing decision points, and asking questions can improve everyday decision making. From now on, each conversation and discussion you are in will likely trigger recognition of decision points, decision styles, ChoiceMark mindsets, hooks and segues, and clarity about whether a decision has actually been made by the end of the discussion.

Chapter Summary

When the team is about to make a bad decision, in my anti-survival role of thinking, it is my responsibility to articulate why the decision is not the right one to make. I can use hooks and segues to share my insights. I also can use hooks and segues to expand my understanding of other people's points of view. Whether the team's final decision is don't do it or proceed with changes, my point of view needs to be heard and understood. Ultimately, a decision made without considering an anti-survival mindset may not be effective and may not be implemented at the level of success at which the team had hoped.

CHAPTER 9

Consensus-Driven Decision Making Versus Command-and-Control Decisions

Which Is Better?

When consensus works, a decision is made and follow-up action occurs. When consensus can't be reached and a decision is still required, more directive options for arriving at a decision, such as command and control, can be invoked. When consensus simply isn't working and timelines are reaching deadline dates, it is time for a decision to be made, which means the approach to decision making may need to change. As you've seen in the Chapters 4 through 8 ChoiceMark practices, there is a beneficial time for shifting from consensus to command-and-control decision making and assignment giving. This chapter is a further discussion of the equal values of consensus and command-and-control decision making as well as an opportunity to identify your organization's decision making culture. At the end of a decision-making process, the sign of a well-made decision is that it supports the organization's mission, leads to achieving agreed-upon goals, and that everyone is clear about what individual responsibilities for implementation are. In other words, regardless of whether consensus or command-and-control decision-making processes are used, the endpoint is an agreement on what actions will be taken, by when and by whom, while maintaining a willingness to continue working together.

When a team's decision processes fail to maintain a willingness to work together, the ability to get work done declines. Sometimes the reduced willingness to work together leads to a complete failure of the project team and ultimately to its being disbanded. Most of the time, however, a lowered willingness to work together raises the amount of conflict that a team experiences. Work still gets done but in a tension-filled environment that is less productive than it could be. Again, the goal is to get a decision made and keep people willing to work together to achieve the organization's mission and goals. Both consensus-driven and command-and-control decision making can lead to this end.

For ten weeks in 2002, I attended the Idaho State Police Academy as a self-sponsored full-time student. I graduated with a sense of accomplishment and with a heightened firsthand understanding of how and when command-and-control communications can work well. Individual assignments, written tests, driving skill tests, weapon retention practices, shooting-range qualifications, and physical fitness tests were required. Teamwork and decision making were required when we moved into scenario practices and responded to calls in an in-action case study approach to handling real calls in the field. The entire academy and the team-based practices were based on the command-and-control model. Someone was always in charge and was the go-to person for all academy questions. During the practices, one person was always the lead officer, making action decisions that supporting officers needed to follow. Whether working alone or in teams in the daily field of police work, there is rarely time for consensus-driven decisions. Being dispatched to a scene requires on-the-spot command decision making for solving problems, improving situations, moving people to safety, and stopping crime.

There Is a Time for Collaborative, Consensus-Driven Decision Making

When large amounts of information and input are needed, collaborative consensus makes sense. Consensus also makes sense when the time frame for decision making doesn't require an immediate decision. When a scheduled approach to gathering information can happen, consensus can work. When people with multiple points of view, varied expertise sets, and a willingness to explore options come together to make a decision, coming to consensus can work. Chapters 2 through 8 covered the value of and the time and place for consensus in great detail.

There Is a Time for Command-and-Control Communications and Decision Making

Nearly two dozen years of emphasis on building teams and collaborative decision making raises this question: "Is there still a place and time for command-and-control style communication and decision making?" Collaboration involves people in discussion and decision-making sessions that usually move forward by coming to consensus. Typically, a large amount of time is needed for the collaborative process to work. Buy-in is usually high because people involved typically have a chance to participate in making the decision.

Command-and-control communications, when effective, also involve others. Here people are involved in gathering information and sharing input that is fed into a hierarchical structure so that multiple points of data can be coordinated. With the input and centralized coordination, the best and most informed options can be explored so that good decisions can be made. In a command-and-control structure, decisions can be made in a short amount of time.

Consider these situations and decide for yourself whether there is a place in our work and personal lives for command-and-control communication.

1. Distracted by a phone call, a mother looks up and out the front window to discover that her three-year-old son is in the middle of the street with an oncoming car. Is there time to come to consensus? Or is a command-and-control tone of voice in order? Clearly a command decision and immediate action is needed to create safety for the child.

2. The fire alarm sounds in the building you work in. Will you call a meeting to decide what needs to be done, or will someone take charge and get everyone out of the building? While this sounds obvious you'd be surprised at the hesitation surrounding "leave-the-building" decisions. A command-and-control plan for evacuation needs to be in place in every workplace (see *Prepared Not Paranoid* [Praeger, 2008] for more information). Direction-givers, floor captains, and the like need to be included in emergency response plans so that employees know whom to turn to for emergency decision making.

3. You are hiking with a friend whom you suddenly discover is terrified of the place and height that you have reached. You can't turn back. Going further up is the best and safest course. Fear has taken over your friend. Can you come to consensus or will taking charge and providing clear directions be best? When fear or concern prevents a person from being able to make rational decisions, someone else needs to step in and provide best-course directions to safer ground, in this case, or to an improved location for discussion.

4. Your front office has just received a bomb threat. Will you have time to form a committee? Or what plan will you put into action? Who will take control? Similar to situation 2 above, this situation demands that one person be in charge and give clear directions regarding what is to happen next. Command-and-control decision making often relies on existing plan, policy, and decision-making documents as well as on-the-spot assessments of which parts of the plans to implement.

Given just these four examples, clearly the answer is, "Yes, there is a time to implement command-and-control decisions and communications." Whenever life is threatened, use a command-and-control approach. Whenever the organizational agreement is to use a chain-of-command decision process, rely on command and control. Each time a deadline is near and a team is deadlocked in indecision, consider a shift to command-and-control direction giving and decision making. On the other hand, when does command and control not work well or work against the good of the group's mission? Command-and-control decision approaches fail to work whenever the person in the command position takes so much control of a situation that information is not gathered from the field. The field, frontline workforce, or research teams are where real-time and real-life information is found. Without good field intelligence, marketplace knowledge and staff input, poor decisions get made.

Both command-and-control and consensus-driven processes are only effective when people have expertise and competence to gather information and to act upon it; those involved in decision discussions willingly share information and expertise; the person or group making the final decision has used all the information available to make good decisions; everyone involved has strong listening, speaking, observation, and question-asking skills; and, lastly, the person or group making the final decision actually has the authority to make the decision.

Tools for Making Decisions

Develop your skills with command-and-control as well as consensus-driven communications and decision making. There is a place, even a demand for both in our daily workplaces and lives. Some of the tools associated with command-and-control and consensus-driven communications are described in the following paragraphs. Whichever tool or combination of tools you and your team choose to use in a decision discussion, use communication approaches that maintain people's willingness to work together.

Consensus is the result of coming together to reach an agreement. To reach consensus a variety of discussion and information-gathering tools can be used. For instance, the ChoiceMark stages for consensus described here in *Moving Out of the Box* are powerful, discussion-expanding tools for leading to a final decision. The process of reaching a consent agreement can use also such tools as brainstorming to gather ideas, information gathering tied to budgets and financial analysis, Pareto chart analysis, and work planning that relates to agreed-upon project management timelines.

Some decision discussion tools are associated with both consensus-driven and command-and-control decision making. For instance, prioritizing or ranking a series of solutions can happen during a consensus-driven discussion and can happen during a command-and-control debate. Pros and cons are often explored in both approaches to decision making as a form of gathering information about what will allow the solution to work and work well in addition to what could cause the solution to cause harm. Decision tree and workflow analysis can be applied also in multiple decision making approaches.

Command-and-control decision making results from one or a limited number of people making a final decision based on input fed up to them through a chain-of-command system of communications. The tools used in a variety of decision-making approaches that really come from the command-and-control end of the decision continuum include voting; ranking and prioritizing; order giving; assignment giving; gathering and assessing information about the urgency of the problem to be solved; and gathering information about and assessing the importance of the decision at hand. When people working to come to consensus get frustrated, an often heard suggestion that comes from command-and-control decision making is, "Let's take a vote to see where we are." Taking a vote to discover whether a majority exists in favor of or against a decision is a command action. Taking a vote and then returning to a come-to-consensus discussion can work to reach a decision with as much buy-in as possible and yet it can also backfire. Taking a vote and then carrying on the consensus discussion appears to many team members as waffling. Be aware that once a vote is taken, many team members are ready to move on rather than sit still for further discussions.

Use Command and Control Without Alienating Others

As you've likely gathered from the preceding discussions, while there is an appropriate time to use command-and-control decision making, it is a decision approach than can alienate and offend others. When an organization's culture is clearly based on command-and-control decision making, assignment giving, and information sharing, individual employees are more comfortable with and accepting of command decisions. Conversely, when an organization's culture is driven by consensus-based decisions, a shift to command decisions can disrupt problem solving and alienate team members from participating in decision implementation.

The key to successfully applying command-and-control decision making that results in implementation actions is two-fold. First, know when to use command and control. There is a time and a place, as you've read throughout *Moving Out of the Box*. Second, use command-and-control decision making in a manner that is respectful to every person in the organization. When urgency of action is demanded, such as in an emergency safety situation, people are less likely to be offended if someone seems abrupt or rude in their decision making and direction giving. When direction giving and question asking happen in a respectful tone of voice and in a respectful demeanor, people are less likely to be offended too. Some of the ways to show respect during command-and-control decision making processes include using effective communication skills, tones of voice, and body language; spending a reasonable amount of time listening to expert and relevant input; making a clear decision that people know how to act upon; giving directions in the form of suggestions rather than orders; and making yourself available should questions or challenges arise.

Conflict Resolution and Decision Making

When entrenched on either side of neutral, individual team members can contribute to conflict-filled team interactions. Because of the degrees of passion and commitment to their individual points of view, each of the four mindsets on either side of neutral can so poorly listen to others that the result is some level of conflict. And because decision-making discussions often demand that opposing points of view be discussed before a final decision is reached, it is often inevitable that some level of tension or outright conflict will occur during the discussion. While each ChoiceMark mindset can create limited listening ability, each ChoiceMark mindset can contribute these conflict-resolving strengths to a decision making discussion. Extreme excitement contributes an optimistic outlook that says "everything is possible." Engaged enthusiasm contributes an attitude for positive problem resolution and a decision to take action. Neutral contributes a willingness to hear all points of view in order to find a common or middle ground that can work fairly well for everyone. Boxed-in contributes an ability to identify problems that can prevent the solution from working. And the anti-survival mindset contributes an ability to point out any harmful consequences that might result from making the decision as proposed. All five points of view are needed in the final consensus-driven decision so that the best-possible decision is reached. Again, some levels of conflict and tension are inevitable during a decision-making process. The key is not to get stuck in the conflict. Instead, work to enlarge each decision-making discussion with the Choice-Mark tools and then to reach a decision based on best-possible information and input.

The Organization's Culture for Decision Making

In Chapter 2, you discovered your personal approaches to making decisions, consensus, waffling, command and control, and your preferred mindset for consensus. Teams, committees, business divisions, boards of directors, and organizations guided by missions that must be achieved are called upon to make decisions. Otherwise, these work units would not exist. Just as individuals have preferred styles of decision making, so too do work units. Recall the Chapter 1 story about the meeting culture that never resulted in decision making. Now you can recognize that this culture is one of waffling because no clear decisions result and therefore no clear action items and work assignments result. In the survey that follows, you can discover what your organization's preferred and predominant decision-making culture is. To identify the decision-making style of your team, division, board or organization, respond to the following survey.

Organizational Decision-Making Survey

Which of the following happen in your organization—and with what frequency? First, put a checkmark in the "Happens" column if the process listed ever happens in your organization. Then, in the "How Often?" column, circle the frequency at which you experience the process in your organization. (Note: Don't worry about the category name for now—you'll fill that in after completing the survey.)

Happens? How Often?

Category A:_____

	Happens?	How Often?
1. Collaboration	_____	Daily / Weekly / Monthly / Rarely
2. Brainstorming	_____	Daily / Weekly / Monthly / Rarely
3. Idea Generation	_____	Daily / Weekly / Monthly / Rarely
4. Problem solving processes.	_____	Daily / Weekly / Monthly / Rarely
5. Exploring and agreeing on solutions.	_____	Daily / Weekly / Monthly / Rarely

6. ChoiceMark tool is implemented. _____ Daily / Weekly / Monthly / Rarely

7. Tools for reaching consensus are _____ Daily / Weekly / Monthly / Rarely
   used.

8. Pro and Con charts are generated. _____ Daily / Weekly / Monthly / Rarely

9. Idea prioritization occurs. _____ Daily / Weekly / Monthly / Rarely

10. Compromise. _____ Daily / Weekly / Monthly / Rarely

11. Reaching agreement. _____ Daily / Weekly / Monthly / Rarely

12. Listening to many ideas. _____ Daily / Weekly / Monthly / Rarely

13. Teams have authority to make _____ Daily / Weekly / Monthly / Rarely
    decisions.

14. We are all in charge, no one _____ Daily / Weekly / Monthly / Rarely
    person has responsibility.

Total Checked: Total Circled

_____ _____ _____ _____ _____

Happens? How Often?

Category B:_____

1. Failure to make a decision. _____ Daily / Weekly / Monthly / Rarely

2. Putting off a decision and never _____ Daily / Weekly / Monthly / Rarely
   returning to the discussion to
   make a decision.

3. Indicating that the right people _____ Daily / Weekly / Monthly / Rarely
   are not present for the decision
   to be made, and yet never having
   the right people present.

4. Relying on someone else to _____ Daily / Weekly / Monthly / Rarely
   make a decision such that a
   decision never gets made

5. Revisiting a decision repeatedly   _____   Daily / Weekly / Monthly / Rarely
   after it has been made

6. Delaying decisions indefinitely   _____   Daily / Weekly / Monthly / Rarely

7. Constant requests for more data   _____   Daily / Weekly / Monthly / Rarely

8. Continuous research-phases   _____   Daily / Weekly / Monthly / Rarely
   that don't lead to decision

9. Team discussions don't lead to   _____   Daily / Weekly / Monthly / Rarely
   decisions

10. Teams don't have authority to   _____   Daily / Weekly / Monthly / Rarely
    make the decisions they are
    asked to make

11. When a decision is made   _____   Daily / Weekly / Monthly / Rarely
    without certain people, the
    decision gets undone later

12. Unwillingness to make decisions _____   Daily / Weekly / Monthly / Rarely
    costs our organization money

13. Unwillingness to make decisions _____   Daily / Weekly / Monthly / Rarely
    causes us to lose customers

14. No one really knows who is in   _____   Daily / Weekly / Monthly / Rarely
    charge

Total Checked: Total Circled

_____ _____ _____ _____ ____

Happens? How Often?

Category C: _____

1. Decisions are made and   _____   Daily / Weekly / Monthly / Rarely
   work gets done

2. Votes are taken to make a   _____   Daily / Weekly / Monthly / Rarely
   decision

3. Assignment giving occurs without _____ Daily / Weekly / Monthly / Rarely
   discussion or volunteerism

4. We have a clear chain of _____ Daily / Weekly / Monthly / Rarely
   command

5. In emergency situations, clear and _____ Daily / Weekly / Monthly / Rarely
   immediate directions are given

6. In emergency situations, after _____ Daily / Weekly / Monthly / Rarely
   directions are given, action
   immediately follows

7. Assignments or orders that are _____ Daily / Weekly / Monthly / Rarely
   nondebatable and nonnegotiable
   are given

8. A limited number of people are _____ Daily / Weekly / Monthly / Rarely
   authorized to make decisions

9. Conflict is handled quickly _____ Daily / Weekly / Monthly / Rarely

10. Everyone knows who is in _____ Daily / Weekly / Monthly / Rarely
    charge

11. SWOT analysis is done (SWOT _____ Daily / Weekly / Monthly / Rarely
    is strengths, weaknesses,
    opportunities, and threats)

12. Once decisions are made, we _____ Daily / Weekly / Monthly / Rarely
    move forward

13. Work teams are clearly defined _____ Daily / Weekly / Monthly / Rarely

14. Consequences for choices are _____ Daily / Weekly / Monthly / Rarely
    clear when individual decisions
    are made

Total Checked: Total Circled

_____ _____ _____ _____ _____

Scoring Directions

If you haven't already, for each of the three categories above, enter your total number of checkmarks on the "Total Checked" line. Next add up the number of "Daily" circles in the "Daily" column and enter this total on the first "Total Circled" line. Then do the same for the columns labeled "Weekly," "Monthly," and "Rarely"; add up the number of circles in each column and enter the totals on the corresponding "Total Circled" lines. Now, return to the category heading and write the word Consensus on the line after Category A. Then enter the word Waffler on the line after Category B. Finally, add the words Command and Control on the line after Category C. Given the 14 questions in each category, you are probably not surprised by these headings.

Now that you have totals, in each of the three named categories, add the Total Checked point total to the Total Circled Daily column point total and write this number in the space in between these two lines. Circle the highest of these three numbers and look at which category heading, Consensus, Waffling or Command and Control, the number is under. The heading with the highest number indicates the predominate decision-making culture in your organization.

If two of the three numbers are within one point of each other, these two decision-making cultures are at work in your organization. If all three numbers are within one point of each other, one of two things is occurring: (a) each of the three decision-making approaches is being used in appropriate situations and is leading to consistently productive results, or (b) none of the three decision-making approaches are being effectively used in your organization and confusion and lost productivity is resulting. You know your organization best; is it "a" or "b"? Because it can't be both.

Survey Debriefing

When an organization has a predominant decision-making culture, the people working in the organization get used to and even comfortable with that approach because if they don't they'll typically quit to work for another organization. By identifying the decision culture daily at work in the organization, leaders can better serve and fulfill the organization's mission. When leaders understand decision tools, master both consensus and command-and-control processes, and can easily maneuver between the decision-making approaches, decisions are made more effectively and in a more timely manner. Just as individuals with preferred decision-making styles have strengths and limitations, so does the decision-making culture of an organization.

Consensus and Collaboration: Organizations with a predominant decision culture in the realm of consensus and collaboration find strength in gathering decision input from multiple points of view. Making a consensus-driven decision takes the organization longer than making a command-and-control decision. However, unlike a waffling organizational culture, a decision does get made. The limitations to a consensus-driven organization are that it takes longer to make decisions which can sometimes cause missed opportunities and missed deadlines. When a repeated failure to reach consensus lead repeatedly to waffling, consensus discussions have created a frustration in the culture that can lead to disengagement and even to quitting the organization.

Waffling: Organizations living with a waffling culture typically miss critical deadlines, fail to make timely decisions, miss opportunities for improvement and growth, and even lose customers. There is not one strength in having a consistently waffling decision culture. There are only limitations and downsides. If your organization scored highest in the waffling category, get everyone on your team and in the organization to read *Moving Out of the Box* so that the culture can change to a clear decision-making culture that can utilize both consensus and command-and-control decision making.

Command and Control: Organizations with an overriding command-and-control culture typically are found in the military, law enforcement, and industries related to them, as well as in governmental agencies. The strength of an organizational command-and-control decision-making culture is that everyone knows who is in charge. Additional strengths include the ability to make decisions quickly and to keep moving forward with implementation. The limitations to a command-and-control culture are that creativity can be diminished, everyone does not get input on a decision, and a sense of not being listened to can grow into detachment from projects and even quitting to leave the organization.

When People Want Command-and-Control Decision Making

When situations are confusing, discussions drag on without conclusion, or when life seems threatened, people want someone to take charge, give directions, and get things done. Most people prefer to live with a sense of order and clarity that prevents chaos from taking hold. As a result, reaching a decision, whatever the decision is, can become so important that people not only don't care what the final decision is, but also they tend not to care how the final decision is made. When stress is running high, when a break has been taken and the team has regrouped but decisions are still not getting made, it is time for a change in the decision process. Move to command and control to make a decision recommendation and begin the implementation planning.

For example, during the September 11, 2001, attack on the World Trade Center Towers, a security guard took charge. He had worked in the towers during the early 1990s bombing and the story makes clear that having a command plan of action in an emergency made a difference. This security guard directed and even ordered people to leave their desks and their offices to get out of and away from the tower to safety. He had studied the building structures and had an understanding of what a bomb could do to take down the buildings. People in panic tend to forget how to make decisions. They'll forget where the stairs are or forget where the exit doors are located even though they walk through them or past them every workday. A security guard's job is to keep people safe and this guard knew that giving direct orders to leave the building was the best way to keep people safe. A more in-depth discussion of the need for community building at work to create a more safe environment is found in my book *Building Community in Buildings* (Praeger, 2007).

In the aftermath of the April 2007 deadly shootings of students at Virginia Tech, the school was criticized for not having a clear command-and-control emergency procedure in place. Whether or not the school had a clear procedure in place, the perception that it didn't and that the failure to take control of communications to keep students safe lead to great distress and discussion about what to do in future situations. Emergency situations are easily the most identifiable times when people want a command-and-control order for decision making and communications.

Command-and-control decision making works well for crowd control, traffic control, emergency response and management, as well as crisis handling. Each of these situations requires clear directions, immediate response, and confident leadership that moves people to safety. In addition to emergency situations, people want a command-and-control decision to be made when the timing of a decision is critical and it seems like the deadline will be missed. Generally, people are aware when a discussion has gone on too long and that it is time for a decision. However, when people don't have, or feel they don't have, authority to make a decision, they look to the person(s) with authority and expect a command-and-control decision to be made. To shift to command and control without alienating others, use a tone of voice that is respectful and offer a clear statement of reasons for the shift to command and control. Typically an urgency factor is what drives a shift to command-and-control decision making. Once the urgency of a situation has diminished, a shift or return to consensus-driven discussions and decision making can occur.

Decision Meeting Venues

Decision making happens on the part of individuals and teams. Decision making sometimes happens in an instant and often happens after research, study, and reflection. Sometimes the research phase for a final design in the workplace, in the courts, or in our personal lives can last for years. The discussions held during decision making can happen in our own thinking, in meeting rooms, on telephone calls, and in virtual meeting environments. During the early 1990s, the first widely available video conferencing installations allowed people in different locations to talk with each other at the same time. Video conferencing didn't quite take hold due to the slow-motion video and already challenged meeting and decision-making skills. Teleconferencing became a more common venue for people in different locations to talk together at the same time. In the 2000s, Internet-driven meetings with live-time conversation and document sharing became popular. Also in the 2000s, telepresence systems such as Hewlett Packard's Halo Collaboration Studio make meeting face-to-face, even when you are in different locations, seem like you really are in the same room. Telepresence refers to television quality video streaming live-time with no delayed movement or audio that makes you feel you are in the presence of the person you see on the video screen.

Hewlett Packard and DreamWorks collaboratively partnered to create the Halo telepresence collaboration solution for meetings. Having experienced the seamless technology of the Halo system myself, Halo and systems like it appear poised to revolutionize multi-site technology-connected meeting rooms. The technology is finally transparent so that meeting participants feel as though they are in the same room even though they may be 10,000 miles apart. In addition to the fully in-person feeling of the room design, Halo runs on a global fiber optic backbone network dedicated to only Halo traffic. The Halo system is driven by one mouse and collaboration software that operates on a separate screen from the meeting partici-pant video screens so that the ease of use keeps people focused on the discussions at hand. Laptops can be hooked into the meeting room technology too so that docu-ments and visuals can be viewed by participants in the multiple locations. And with 24-hour, 7-day-a-week managed support, a meeting can happen any time of day or night any place in the world where the Halo rooms exist. The types of decision-making meetings that Hewlett Packard is finding Halo to be most used for include interviews; virtual team management and work planning meetings; product develop-ment; research and development; performance reviews; and managers coaching employee performance on an ongoing basis.

Many decision discussions will remain dependent on face-to-face interactions. With telepresence systems, travel time and expenses can be dramatically reduced, thereby protecting work-time for each person involved in the decision discussion. As companies of all sizes open and maintain offices in multiple and often distant locations, being able to hold decision-making discussions without leaving the office and without loosing travel time will become increasingly important. Ultimately, whatever the venue or meeting location, the mastery of the decision-making approaches presented in *Moving Out of the Box* is critical to successful and effective decision making.

Chapter Summary

Whatever the predominant decision-making culture your organization has, there are opportunities to improve individual and team mastery of decision-making tools, approaches, and mindsets. The premise for *Moving Out of the Box* remains the same: both command-and-control and consensus-driven decision making have equal value because they each have an appropriate time and place for most-effective use. When the decision culture of an organization prevents decisions from being made, prevents creativity and productivity from flourishing, and prevents an ongoing willingness on the part of team members to work together, it is time for individual mastery of ChoiceMarks language and an overall change in the decision culture.

CHAPTER **10**

Which ChoiceMark Is Your Worldview?

Worldviews and Decision Making

Decision making happens as a result of people bringing their experiences, opinions, expertise, points of view, and ideas to the discussion table. Leaving all of these things out of the discussion creates a decision vacuum in which critical information, experience, and creative thinking are missing. Whether making professional or personal decisions, more information than ever is available for consideration. The challenge mentioned in the first chapter of this book is that we get so overloaded with information these days that it is difficult to find the relevant and useful information upon which to build a decision. Some of the filters for sorting information come from experience, cultural exposure, points of view, and studied expertise. Additional filters for accepting information at discussion tables include levels of trust and worldviews that are also described as outlooks on life.

For example, some cultures give trust to others until something happens for the trust to be withdrawn. Other cultures expect trust to be earned, which means some people may never be granted with a position of trust because they never earn it. The level of trust placed with an individual affects other people's ability to listen to and interact with that person when in conversation and especially when making decisions. When there is no trust, no confident decision making for positive action can occur. When there is trust, decision making can occur with a hope for positive implementation to follow. On another front, does your worldview take "an eye for an eye" or "turn the other cheek" approach to interacting with others? This consideration matters because when you feel wronged, or even simply let down, by someone else the decisions you make going forward will be based on revenge or on forgiveness. An eye for an eye mentality is one of revenge. A turn the other cheek mentality is one of forgiveness. When someone doesn't follow through on a commitment or a promise your reaction at the time of the letdown as well as at future times of interaction and decision making can affect the outcomes of the discussions being held and of the decisions to be made

Life experience can dictate decision comfort zones. Have you ever spoken to a person who recently left military service and upon returning to civilian life felt that civilians live chaotic, unordered, and undisciplined lives? Years ago I heard this comment during an in-flight conversation with another passenger. What it speaks to is how life experiences affect people's perceptions of how things happen, how things should happen, and how people want things to happen. Military and law enforcement life certainly prepares people to comfortably handle command-and-control decision environments. Even lives lived in religious orders, convents, temples, and societies lend to comfort with the hierarchy of command-and-control decision cultures. Conversely, working in corporate cultures dedicated to team-based work and decision making lends itself to having a comfort with consensus-driven decision making.

A willingness to take risks also affects decision comfort zones. Most people in command-and-control cultures are not taking great risks in decision making because they are primarily carrying out decisions authorized by others. People working in consensus-driven environments are taking risks each time the team makes a decision as well as each time the team delays or fails to make a decision. So a higher amount of comfort with risk taking is needed from everyone participating in consensus-driven decisions. Without a willingness to take risks, nearly all decisions would result in maintaining the status quo. And no longer status quo is the emphasis on command-and-control approaches in governmental agency decision making. While command and control continues to be in force, over the last decade there has been a growing emphasis on consensus. Governmental agencies at federal, state, and local emphasis are ever more focused on public input and consensus. When monies get directed to projects, there is increasingly a focus on gathering community input that can lead to a consensus for action to be taken. From road projects to community art projects, coming to consensus is a part of the requirements for receiving the monies.

Stop Getting Stuck

You know your team is stuck making a decision when any one of the following or even a combination of the following occurs. All talk and no decision making prevails during team meetings. People leave meeting discussions before reaching a decision. Some team members no longer show up to meetings because they say no conclusions are ever reached. Meetings never end with a decision. Meeting endings do not include a summary of who is going to do what by when, causing the next meeting to be a repeat of the last one. Meeting leaders are not in control of meetings and don't get the team to make a decision. Once a decision is made, it seems to be undone or redone about half of the time.

Teams get stuck decision making for a variety of reasons. Sometimes one individual brings decision making to a halt. Someone with authority to halt a decision who randomly exercises that authority can leave a team feeling stuck and wasting time. Someone with great concerns also can bring a meeting decision process to a halt when no one else has any suggestions for overcoming concerns. Other times subsets of team members prevent a decision from being made. Still other times the whole team agrees not to make a decision during the meeting. Over two decades of working with teams leads to the following list of primary reasons that teams break down in their attempts to make a decision.

First, when the purpose of decision is not clear meeting participants struggle with why time needs to be spent discussing something that makes no sense. Related to this, when results, outcomes, and consequences of a decision are not clear, people tend to avoid reaching agreement or making a decision that leads to implementation. Third, when working in the spirit of reaching team consensus, there is a real danger of talking things to death, without reaching a decision. And fourth, when the timing of the decision making wasn't clear up front, team members grow frustrated with a process that seems to be taking too long, or grow angry when pushed to make a decision in a time frame that seems unrealistically short. Team decision breakdown reasons one through four have to do with the process and structure of effective meeting conduct. These breakdowns can be fixed by strengthening meeting conduct skills and processes.

Decision breakdown reasons five and six are interpersonal challenges that may or may not be able to be overcome by a team. The fifth reason team decision making tends to break down is distrust and dislike. Not often talked about openly, the lack of willingness to work together that results from interpersonal distrust and dislike is at work in many teams. Reluctance to share information in a meeting can be a sign of distrust. Outright name calling (which a few clients over the years have described as regular occurrences in the team meetings that lead up to bringing in an outside facilitator) is a sign of both distrust and dislike. And failure to follow through on assignments can also be a sign of distrust and dislike being at work in a team. Breakdown five can be overcome by working one-on-one with team members to get to the root of the problem, reach resolution, and rebuild team relationships. Sometimes this effort is not enough and an executive coach is needed for every member of the team so that individual skills improve and before the team will be able to reach agreement on effective decisions.

And breakdown reason number six is outright conflict at the discussion table. When distrust and dislike issues go unresolved it is inevitable that the team will fall apart or that conflict will arise. When conflict flares up without announcement, it may be the sign of a momentary disagreement that is powerful but surmountable. And when conflict persists, it is the sign of larger unrest with or distrust over the team's interpersonal dynamics, overall purposes, or overall inability to achieve its purposes. Conflict can be overcome by selecting from a variety of approaches the one that is most appropriate for the team. Again one-on-one meetings or executive coaching is an option. An outside, professional facilitator can lead a team at a low level of conflict through it, the tasks needing to be addressed, and the decisions needing to be made. When a high level of conflict exists, a mediator can be brought in to help a group or team reach a decision. Over the last nearly 100 years, mediation has particularly been used in union and management negotiations. Whatever approach is taken to resolving interpersonal challenges there are two endpoints: get a decision made that can be implemented and rebuild the team members' willingness to work together or the team will have to be rebuilt.

One high-tech client of mine brought me in for a two-day facilitated meeting because the team was unable to get through a tactical planning agenda on its own. Twice during the first day I called the meeting to a halt saying, "I can get you through the agenda. However, you each need to make a decision as to whether you are committed to working together through this agenda." The first time I said this, the team committed to working through the agenda and we moved on with the work before the team. The second time the team stumbled, I repeated the same sentence and added, "I can get you through this agenda. However, if there are unresolved issues that prevent each of you from working this agenda then we need to end this meeting, and someone who can help you work through the deep dark issues involved here needs to come in to help." Then, I had everyone leave the room and return with their personal answer in 15 minutes. All team members returned and opted to keep working together on the original agenda. Day one of the two-day retreat accomplished the task decisions that were on the agenda. Midway through day two, another breakdown occurred and yet again the team members stuck it out to end up with about 25 action items for the upcoming three-month period of work. The ongoing challenge for this team is the unresolved past behaviors that haven't been overcome nor have the hurts caused been let go of. My final recommendation to the team was that they each work with an executive coach to overcome the communication and behavioral challenges that lead to the team even needing to bring in an outside facilitator.

Again, task, process, and structural challenges are easiest to overcome as long as team and meeting leaders commit to gaining skills in meeting conduct, problem solving, and decision making. The more difficult challenges to overcome are indeed the interpersonal ones because they require personal reflection on and response to the question, "Am I willing to continue working with this team or is it time for me to move to another team?" Individual team members are the only ones who can answer this question. When people like the work they are doing, answering the question becomes more difficult. On a personal front, the same question arises in these forms: "Am I willing to continue doing all the work to maintain this friendship, or is it time to let it go?" or, "Am I willing to continue being treated this way in this relationship, or is it time for me to leave because all efforts to improve the situation have not worked?" Interpersonal differences, conflicts, and outright refusal to work to make situations better prompt difficult decisions to be made about the configuration of teams and personal relationships.

Preferred ChoiceMarks Influence Your Worldview

The phrase "worldview" refers to what your perspective frames of reference are as you live your life, as you interact with others, and as you make decisions. Some would say the "half-full or half-empty glass" discussion describes a person's outlook and worldview. Others suggest that being an optimist or a pessimist describes your worldview. Still others say that thinking of yourself as a victim is a worldview, or mindset, that affects how the world is viewed and how interactions with the world occur. Many descriptive phrases exist to help describe points of view, mindsets, outlooks, attitudes, and worldviews. And more than a few would say, all of these outlooks and viewpoints combine to create a person's worldview. "Take your blinders off" is a phrase used to encourage people to see more perspectives than those they are currently focused on. And the phrase "cut me some slack" is a request for some latitude to play with ideas, to present new options, or to be given a chance where usually someone gets cut off.

Now add into the worldview mix your preferred decision-making style, consensus, waffling, or command and control, and your preferred ChoiceMark mindset and worldview perspectives expand yet again. Described in terms of worldviews, here are the eight decision tools *Moving Out of the Box* has focused upon. A consensus mindset for decision making views the world as a place where everyone can come together to reach agreements on things that are good for everyone. Whereas a waffling mindset rests in or worries in a place of indecision hoping that others will make decisions they the wafflers can live with. Next, the command-and-control mindsets' worldview is one of order, structure, clear authority, and not crossing the lines of authority. Each decision-making style brings a different worldview to the discussion table.

Each of the ChoiceMark mindsets also views the world from different perspectives. As you read through the following descriptions, consider whether your preferred ChoiceMark stage of consensus is also your preferred ChoiceMark point of view. Extreme excitement views the world as full of possibilities to become passionate about. Engaged enthusiasm sees the world as full of potential options to pursue. Neutral views the world as neither good nor bad, neither interesting nor uninteresting, and neither worth getting involved with nor staying away from. Boxed-in looks out into a world of limited options many of which have been tried before and have failed. And anti-survival sees the world as full of danger that can be avoided if people would just pay attention. Whatever your worldview, you have the power to choose what point of view you work from when making decisions and to choose whether you'll willingly shift mindsets during the decision making process.

Shifting Mindsets without Losing Your Identity

In Chapter 2, you discovered whether you have an affinity for one decision style over the others. And just now you've checked whether the ChoiceMark viewpoint for looking at the world matches up with your preferred ChoiceMark stage of reaching consensus. Your preferred decision-making approach may be so much a part of you that you associate it with your personal identity. Your decision-making approach doesn't have to define who you are or what your identity is. If you had a single high point score on the Chapter 2 Decision-Making Style Survey, others may perceive that decision style as a part of your identity too. Again, it doesn't have to be. Now that you've identified your preferred decision making style and improved your decision making discussion skills with the ChoiceMarks, you can recognize tools and skills for making decisions rather than incorporating a single tool into your identity. As you've discovered, each decision-making style has strengths. The key to shifting mindsets for decision making is to focus on the strengths of each style. The strength of the command-and-control style is making a decision now. The waffler strength plays out when more data really is needed and a specific time has been agreed upon to come back to the discussion and reach a decision that can be implemented. And the strength of the consensus style is gathering input from multiple points of view to gain the most buy-in possible for both the making of the decision and its implementation.

Shifting mindsets for decision making is next largely dependent on the two factors of timing for a shift and mastering each of the decision-making approaches. The timing of making a shift is important because shifting abruptly from a consensus-oriented process to command and control can break the trust of a team. Timing considerations are also important because a decision-making culture driven by command-and-control decisions making an abrupt change to "now we do things by consensus" is unlikely to be successful because an unprepared mindset and a lacking skill set for consensus will prevent the transition. Use these guidelines for shifting from one mindset to another and for increasing the likelihood of success.

Shift from waffling to consensus when conversations need to be expanded to gather enough information to make a decision. Shift to consensus when time allows for the expanded discussion and when team members are willing to share their expertise to help arrive at a decision. Staying in waffling mode just aggravates individuals and prevents the team from reaching a conclusive decision for action.

Shift from waffling to command and control when the time for making a decision is now. In other words, when no more time for debate and discussion is available, shift to command-and-control direction giving for implementation. Again, staying in waffling mode just aggravates individuals and prevents a conclusive decision for action from being made.

Shift from consensus to command and control when time for decision making has run out or when no clear consensus is likely to be reached. Talking things through without reaching a conclusion is a form of waffling. When tension is high, or tempers have flared, even a momentary move to commanding a break be taken, "Let's take a 20-minute break right now and then come back to decide what to do," can be an appropriate shift. A longer-term shift from consensus to command and control may be required when timing is so tight that further discussion is unreasonable and when an implementation plan requires many time sensitive assignments to be carried out. Once the urgent situation has been handled, a return to consensus-reaching may be appropriate.

Shift from command and control to consensus when urgent decision making is no longer needed or when safety concerns have been resolved. A shift to consensus also can reasonably occur when authority lines are clearly established and vast information gathering is a priority. Command and control decision-making organizational cultures typically have difficulty shifting to consensus-driven decision making until an organization-wide investment is made in gaining consensus-reaching skills, establishing team authority levels, and in improving the conduct of decision making meetings. Individuals, team members, and team leaders have the power to guide the balanced use of command-and-control and consensus-driven decision making. And individuals and teams have the power to shift organizational decision-making cultures by beginning with the team currently in place. Once successes are seen, others pay attention to what made the successes happen.

Others' Worldviews Influence Us

Whether or not we actively allow other people's thinking to influence us, it does. Advertisements, newscasts, newspaper stories and columns, television programs, workshops, classes, coaching sessions, sporting events, theater events, concerts, grocery trips, shopping trips, vacations, commute-time radio listening—everything we do and see on a daily basis has the potential to influence our thinking. The challenge is to become clear about what we believe and value so that we know what to say "yes" to allowing into our thinking and decision-making processes. When there is a lack of clarity about personal values, beliefs, and goals, it is easy to be taken advantage of by people who are clear about the factors that drive their decision making and requests. When personal values and beliefs are clear, decision making becomes easier to manage in a timely and clear-cut manner that prevents waffling and indecision.

Consider the following quotes and how they can influence the way individual and team decisions are made. Some of the quotes are from well-known figures, others are from meeting room posters, and still other quotes that influence our thinking are from anonymous sources. All of these ideas have the capacity to influence the way a decision is made.

1. From William Shakespeare's play *As You Like It:* "All the world's a stage, and all the men and women merely players. They have their exits and their entrances; and one man in his time plays many parts." Shakespeare's thinking and viewpoints are alive in today's workplace, community, and cultural event environments. The above quote can influence daily decision making because it offers the mindset of "the world being bigger than the people who show up in it and who have such a small role to play." This first mindset demonstrated in the quote suggests that as decision makers we have small parts to play in the larger scheme of things. You decide whether you agree with this. I for one don't because I do believe in the power of one person's question, statement, or suggestion to change how things turn out. The second mindset from the above quote is one of "even in their comings and goings, each person plays many parts during his life." This can be tied to several decision-making components,

including the decision approach and ChoiceMark preferences that are "parts" of how decisions get made.

2. From Albert Einstein: "Intuition is more important than knowledge." Whether or not you agree with this sentiment, the quote relates to the ChoiceMark stages of extreme excitement and anti-survival. Intuition can be one of the causes for believing without a doubt that something will work and should be pursued, extreme excitement thinking. Intuition also can be one of the causes for believing beyond doubt that something will cause harm and should not be pursued, snti-survival thinking.

3. "Nobody can make me feel bad without my agreement," said Eleanor Roosevelt. Consensus is based on reaching an agreement. Individuals can give their consent. Team members can give their consent thereby reaching consensus. Roosevelt's message is really a prompt for considering what we give agreement to and that it is always in our power to give that agreement or not. When participating in a decision discussion, determine what you are willing to consider, what you are not willing to consider, and what potential solutions you can support. Identifying each of these things before and during a decision discussion will move the discussion to a more effective decision and do so more quickly.

4. "There is no 'I' in team" is used in newsletters, on meeting room posters, and in book titles. This phrase most certainly creates a mindset and premise for how individuals are asked to participate in teams. The phrase says "put yourself aside, take your personal ego out of the equation, and focus all efforts and energies into the team effort." *Moving Out of the Box* shows that individual thinking is a powerful contributor to team decision making. Again, one person's questions, suggestions, and expertise can change the outcome of a team decision.

5. In 2006, Idaho Superintendent of Education Marilyn Howard said in a public address, "Working together we can sense new possibilities." This nod toward consensus and collaboration suggests the power and creativity of the approaches. Consider what you personally hold to be true about working together. Also consider what your team holds as its value around working together, or working independently and just coming together when required to do so.

6. Jamie Hyneman and Adam Savage of MythBusters fame shared these mindsets while on a 2007 speaking tour. "We are opposite thinkers and yet we work together well as problem solvers." And, "We are acquirers of skills." Opposite and multiple points of view are needed to solve problems and make best-possible decisions. In order to be most effective, consistently acquiring new skills for problem solving, meeting leadership, communication, and decision making is important.

Single sentences can capture concepts that change our points of view. Entire paragraphs can paint pictures that cause us to pause and reconsider our viewpoints. Whatever you allow into your awareness, visually, audibly, or from any sense, influences your thinking and your approach to decision making. You choose. That is the point. You choose how you will gather information, offer ideas, share input, make suggestions, create solutions, solve problems, and make decisions. You choose.

Back to my Police Academy experiences: one Friday afternoon during a weapons retention class we learned about choosing. The primary lesson was about how to hold onto your weapon so that no one can get it away from you. It is your responsibility and should only be used by you as an officer on a scene. The secondary lesson was about choices. Choosing to give up when in a compromised position is an option. So is choosing to not give up and figure out an alternative solution to what appears to be a bad situation. The revelatory moment for me came when during a class practice I was on my knees with my hands up by my ears and my classmate had a red rubber gun to the back of my head. The instructor said: "Even down on your knees with a gun to the back of your head, you have a choice. You can choose to let your life be taken. You can choose to take the situation into your hands and get the gun back into your possession. Or, you can choose to wait the situation out and hope someone will arrive to help you. Today is about knowing that you have options and that you have the power to choose." The same can be said of all decision making. You have choices. You also have the power to take action in support of your positions. In fact, the ever present power to choose was really the primary lesson that Friday at the academy. We all have the power to choose.

Chapter Summary

In a culture where every 30 years "change your thinking and your life will be better" is the message packaged for sale, it is time to add "improved decision-making skills will make your work and life better." Here's why. Having a positive attitude and thinking in terms of the half-full rather than the half-empty can definitely improve your outlook, your life experiences, and reduce your stress levels. This is the start to having a better life. Having a happy and get-what-you-want life is certainly important. However, daily life also consists of making decisions for ourselves, our families, and our work teams. In fact, others ask us to make decisions every day. The decisions may range from, "What do you want to have for lunch?" to "Where do you want to invest this $50,000?" So, the second half of acquiring life-changing skills is to master the skills for making best-possible decisions. Chapter 11 focuses on making decisions and moving forward.

CHAPTER **11**

Make a Decision and Move!

The key to decision making is to make one. Clarify who is responsible for what action and by when, and keep moving forward. Sitting, spinning, debating, reviewing, and never deciding are a waste of time, energy, and resources. Make a decision. Then implement the decision. Clearly day-to-day reality is more difficult than saying "just go get it done." *Moving Out of the Box*'s goal has been to offer decision approach options and ChoiceMarks language that can improve every decision discussion and therefore each decision's implementation. Decision discussions range from handling workplace projects and breakdowns to creating new products and solutions for customers. Personal decision discussions run the gamut of family, financial, housing, big-purchase, and vacation planning. From here on, whatever decision situation you find yourself in, apply the *Moving Out of the Box* strategies for making decisions and moving forward.

Returning to General Brooks' interview, here are some of his suggestions for improved decision making and the balanced use of decision tools and power.

Kemp: What situations can you describe where both consensus and command-and-control approaches were used in the same decision-making sequence?

General Brooks: I ran into this situation innumerable times in the normal course of business. Stop-gap or some type of action needed to be taken as soon as possible without benefit of "staffing" or significant consultation on an issue. I won't go into details except to say action first and talk (negotiation) later. This is particularly the case when multiple agencies are involved and there hasn't been time to consult them.

Kemp: What do you suggest about the use of power?

Brooks: The more power you've got, the more cautious you should be to use it. Sometimes overuse of power can ruin the decision and implementation. And you shouldn't turn people off just because you don't agree with a position. If things get too personal, consider withdrawing from the situation. Making a decision shouldn't be personal, it should be based on what is best for the immediate situation and conditions.

Author note: Think about the General's ever-present positional power. In your organization, who has a clear and ever-present power for making final decisions? If you've just had difficulty identifying such a clear decision maker in your organization, it is likely that a decide-everything-by-consensus culture has become a challenge for your entire organization. Productivity losses tend to result when decision-making authority is not clear. Not to mention the team breakdowns discussed in Chapter 10.

Kemp: What closing recommendations do you have about improved decision making?

Brooks: People today are preoccupied by our entertainment culture and are not learning to think well, interact with each other, or to make sound and reasoned decisions. As I mentioned earlier, look for a mentor who models good decision making. Find a boss who supports and mentors your decision making. In other words, find someone who can help you make good decisions and who won't chew you out if things don't go perfectly. Find someone who will instead mentor you toward a better decision or series of decisions next time.

New Decisions Are Needed

Making one decision is not the end of most decision discussions. Even when it seems like the decision under discussion leads to final and unchangeable results, there is only one circumstance in which things can't be renegotiated or changed, and that is the circumstance that leads to death or the unintended destruction of property. In other words, almost every decision can be followed with implementation and any future decisions will be new ones. Once a decision is made, keep moving. Revisiting a decision made with the best information available at the time keeps the team stuck in the past. Once a decision has been made and implementation has begun, any "revisiting" is really a new discussion because things have changed already. With changed information comes new decision making.

When new information changes the way things need to happen, make a new decision. The closer to the original decision that the new information arrives, the more challenged a team is to not repeat the original discussion and to move forward with the current new decision. The further away from an original decision that new information becomes available, the easier it is to focus on the current situation and new decision making. The reason it is so important to view new information in the framework of making new decisions is that the number of industries is which major technological change happens on a weekly basis has increased in the last decade, making it impossible to "wait for all the information to come in" because then a decision would never get made. Decisions need to be made with all the best information available at the time a decision needs to be made, whether that is today or a week from today. If an attitude of "wait until all of the information is in" prevails, several industries would be stuck in the past and possibly go out of business due to missed opportunities.

New results can also prompt new decisions. Once a decision for change is made, new results, both expected and unexpected, occur. Every time results from an already made decision come in, a new "keep going" or "change things" or "go back to what we were doing" decision arises. When regulatory or environmental changes occur, new decisions are typically required. Another time new decisions are needed is when time frames have changed and the team finds itself with new deadlines. However, just because conditions and situations change, a new decision discussion may not be necessary. Imagine moving into the mindset that every step taken requires a decision. For instance, in the highest level of detail, getting out of bed is a decision; taking the first step out of bed and every step for the rest of the day is a series of decisions; getting ready for the day, eating breakfast, reading the paper, checking emails, driving or commuting to work, going to work—well, you get the idea. Individuals and teams will not get much done with this mindset prevailing. Every day is full of decisions we consciously make once or twice and then we live out those decisions. Each day typically also involves decisions that require discussion with others.

Moving Out of the Box is about the decisions that involve discussion with others. While the tools apply to personal and individual decision making, the focus has been on workplace situations because they are the ones that consume so many hours of each week. Make a decision and move on. In your personal life, you've likely experienced someone who makes a decision and then goes back to debate repeatedly either with you or on their own. In your professional circles, you've likely interacted with someone who seems so utterly unable to make a decision that you've begun avoiding them for fear of your reputation being negatively affected. Decision making is about reaching a conclusion and committing to action that leads somewhere meaningful and productive.

Delaying Decisions Can Be Okay

While waffling and indecision rarely are helpful to the decision-making process, on occasion there are legitimate reasons for delaying a decision. When time is available for more research or extended discussion, a delay that facilitates reaching a better decision in the next meeting is reasonable. When not enough information is available and the additional information is critical to making a good decision, delay the decision to a specific date and make the decision then. When multiple decisions are required of a group, the decision list can be overwhelming. Prioritize the most urgent and critical decisions and handle them first. The lower priority decisions can wait. Finally, it is okay to delay a decision when no harm will come from the delay. In all cases of a delayed decision, a final decision must ultimately be made to move ahead with changes or to leave things as they are.

Putting Decisions into Action

University professor, ethicist, and fellow business author, David Gill says that, "There is a muscle for ethical decision making." I'll build on this metaphor to say that fitness for decision making comes from making decisions. It's just like physical fitness, you only achieve fitness when you take care of yourself and actively exercise.

The more you use your mental capacity and intelligence for gathering and sorting information, analyzing data and options, prioritizing and ranking, idea generation and problem solving, solution generation and decision making, the more capable you are of making best-possible and ever better decisions. In Chapters 4 through 8, the ChoiceMark discussions shed light on how to encourage implementation based on the ChoiceMark mindset a person is in.

When decisions aren't getting made, it is time to refocus the team on the dilemma or issue at hand. Discussions that turn into social conversations are off track. Decision discussions that circle on solutions without prioritizing one or two solutions to take action upon are off course. Team talk that makes meetings last longer than the allotted amount of time derails decision making too. The meeting leader or a participant can bring a discussion back to being on track and productive by using ChoiceMark language from Chapters 3 through 8 and the conversation hooks and segues from Chapter 8. Get a decision made. Once a decision is made, maintenance of existing systems needs to occur, and any new actions agreed upon must also be completed.

Chapters 4 through 8 also presented ideas specific to each ChoiceMark mindset for getting people to participate in decision implementation. Getting people to participate in implementation is similar to getting them to participate in the decision-making process. To encourage successful implementation, use the same end-of-meeting strategies used with people in each ChoiceMark mindset. Before a decision-making meeting ends, be sure to secure commitment for follow-up actions and decision implementation. Also before the end of every meeting, clearly state who is responsible for getting what done and by what deadline. Then, encourage each team member to achieve the result and to let you know if any help or resources are needed along the way. Use phrases such as, "Thanks for taking this on. Let us know what you want help with along the way." When any team members have opted not to participate in implementation, confirm that they will not stand in the way of or interfere with the rest of the team going forward.

Also to ensure decision implementation after the meeting, check in periodically on the progress toward the agreed-upon results. Everyone can sometimes run into frustrations and disappointments that prevent achievement of the original agreed-upon outcomes. Additional between-meeting implementation and follow-through can be invited by using the same phrases: "Just checking in, how are things going? Any problems? Any challenges coming up that we need to address? Let me know if you need anything to get this done. Have you encountered any roadblocks? What can we do to overcome the roadblocks? What successes are you having?" Remember to really pause and listen. When help is most needed is often the time when people are most reluctant to speak up.

In a July/August 2006 *ethix* newsletter, Boeing vice president and chief information officer Scott Griffin said about the future of work, "Emerging technologies around collaboration are going to be key." Recall the Hewlett Packard Halo Collaboration Studio meeting venue discussed in Chapter 6, because every day technologies for collaboration are increasingly available. The real challenge is that people's skill sets for leading effective meetings and decision-resulting discussions are now lagging the technological tools available to speed idea generation and decision making over time and space.

Learn to Balance Command-and-Control and Consensus-Style Decision Making: Scenario Practices

In each of the following meeting moments, determine whether you'd use a command-and-control or consensus-oriented approach for moving the meeting forward. Then circle the hook word or phrase you could use to create a command or ChoiceMark segue to move the meeting discussion forward. In the space after each meeting description, write down what language you would use.

1. What's Going On?

Listen in on this meeting to determine what you'll do to get it back on track.

Meeting Leader Sara: Okay, we're all here. Let's get started. We're already ten minutes late. I called the meeting so we can discuss implementation of sample testing to meet the new federal specifications and labeling requirements.

Gunnar: This affects me and my team. I'll take notes on whatever we decide needs to be done.

Jill: Wait, Bernardo is missing. We need his input on label design to know whether we can fit everything required onto the new labels and then whether the existing packaging will be big enough for the new labels.

Carlos: What is the sample testing that needs to be done? Can't we just follow the guidelines and make new labels?

Jill: No. The specifications Jill mentioned require new test documentation to ensure that all ingredients are included and listed correctly on labels.

Sara: That's right. We are being required to do both new tests and new labels.

Amy: Speaking of food, I'm getting hungry and the cafeteria closes in 20 minutes. I really need lunch.

Questions

1. Will you use a command-and-control or a consensus-oriented approach?

2. What hook words or phrases did you see that you'd use to create a segue and guide the discussion?

3. What will you say to move the meeting forward to a decision?

Potential Answers

1. In this case, either approach can work. Command and control: meeting leader Sara can say, "Okay, we're breaking for lunch and because we have to make progress on this today, come back to the conference room at 1:00 so we can continue." Consensus: meeting leader Sara can say, "What do you all say about breaking for lunch?" and then wait for agreement. Before everyone leaves the room, Sara needs to confirm when the discussion will continue: "What do you think about getting back together at 1:00 to get going on this work?" and then wait for agreement.

2. There are a potential of nine work-related hooks in this short interaction. There are seven neutral hooks are discuss implementation of sample testing; meet the new federal specifications; meet the new labeling requirements; Bernardo is missing; new test documentation; required to do both new tests and new labels; and the cafeteria closes in 20 minutes. And there are two hooks that can be from the mindset of boxed-in and therefore communicating "we're done for now" or from an engaged enthusiasm point of view that is saying "let's move somewhere else." These two hooks are this affects me and my team and getting hungry. Any one of these nine hooks can be turned into a segue that changes the direction of the discussion.

3. As meeting leader, the two choices presented in answer number one are options. As a meeting participant, you can take a consensus-driven position of engaged enthusiasm and offer, "We definitely need a lunch break. What information should we bring back at 1:00 so we can make some decisions?"

2. Nowhere to Run

Rebecca: Who saw the game last night? Did you stay up for all of the overtimes? If you didn't, you sure missed the best plays of the game.

Ted: I missed the game. But did you hear about the shootings on campus? It's yet another tragedy. I don't think I can take much more of this.

Phil: What a waste of talent.

Rebecca: What? What are you talking about Phil?

Phil: I'm talking about the shooter. What a shame that the skills used to commit the crimes weren't applied to something safe and productive.

Lucy: Well, maybe. But we are way off track here. We came to meet about implementing the new claims and service team policy change.

Ralph: More critical is how we'll inform everyone of the changes and how staffing and vacation plans will be affected.

Ken: No, the most critical point is how much money this saves the company.

Lucy: Great, just what employees want to hear from management: "You have more work to do for the same rewards."

Phil: Where is this meeting going? Can we make our decisions and get back to work?

Questions

1. As the meeting leader Rebecca, will you use a command-and-control or a consensus-oriented approach?

2. What hook words or phrases did you see that you'd use to create a segue and guide the discussion?

3. How many worldviews are being expressed in this meeting?

4. What will you say to move the meeting forward to a decision?

Potential Answers

1. Rebecca's team doesn't seem to be in great conflict, which would suggest a command-and-control decision. Nor does her team appear to be working in a command-and-control culture. So, a consensus-oriented approach will make the most sense.

2. There are a potential of 11 hook phrases in this interaction: last night's game; shootings on campus; skills used for something safe, productive and meaningful to society; implementing the new claims and service team policy; inform everyone; inform everyone of the changes; inform everyone of how staffing and vacation plans will be affected; how much money this saves; employees want to hear from management; where is this meeting going; can we make our decisions; and can we get back to work. By themselves, each of these hooks is neutral. However, making a further determination about the mindset of each will depend upon hearing the engaged enthusiasm or boxed-in tone of voice and attitude used to say these things.

3. There are at least seven worldviews expressed in the conversation. Several of them also serve as hooks for moving the discussion forward. The worldviews expressed are sports are of interest; current affairs and news stories such as shootings are of interest; applying skills in a meaningful way is valued; getting work accomplished is valued, "implementing the new claims and service team policy change; people are valued because "we need to inform everyone of changes and how staffing and vacation plans will be affected; money is valued by someone and not necessarily the speaker, in the comment "how much money this saves the company;" and "employees want to hear from management" also is a worldview.

4. Any phrase, sentence, or suggestion that includes the following can work: Acknowledge the desire to move ahead with decisions. Ask team members what they'd like to focus on first: the details of the policy change and how it will work, or how everyone will be informed of the changes. Suggest how you'd like to move forward with the discussion.

3. The Same Old Story

Holly: Let's get started.

Frank: We can't. Harold called the meeting and he's not even here.

Justin: We'll, if we had an agenda we could start without him.

Maureen: True, but we don't. Any idea what the agenda should be?

Lauren: Scheduling the marketing for our new product rollout. That's what we are supposed to be deciding.

Justin: Oh. I didn't bring the right files for that discussion. Looks like I have time to go get them.

Tomas: Oh just stay here. By the time you get back we'll have started and then you really won't know what's going on. Besides, none of the rest of us has the right files either.

Harold: Hi there. Sorry I'm late, got tied up in another meeting.

Questions

1. As a meeting participant, with authority to make team-based decisions, will you use a command-and-control or a consensus-oriented approach?

2. What hook words or phrases did you see that you'd use to create a segue and guide the discussion?

Potential Answers

1. As a meeting participant, Tomas took a command-and-control tone when he said, "Oh just stay here." So depending on your personal style, you could choose to offer another command-type suggestion, or you could stay in consensus mode and offer, "We're all here now. Why don't we focus on the marketing schedule."

2. There are three relevant hooks: agenda; scheduling the marketing; and the new product rollout. Again, by themselves, these hooks are neutral. In order to determine which of the remaining four ChoiceMarks might be in action, we'd need to hear the tone of voice and attitude used to deliver the words and statements.

4. No Time Left

Eight people are in a weekly sales meeting for the purpose of working together to close client deals. Rene is the team leader.

Marge: My client wanted our proposal two days ago. We stand the risk of losing this bid because we haven't even submitted one.

Mike: I got back to you with what you said you needed: price-points for each of the quantities you listed.

Marge: Right, you did and thanks. But I never got back the specification documentation I asked for or the information about custom color and client logo additions on each part. Can't anyone help me with this?

Questions

1. Would you use a command-and-control or a consensus-oriented approach?

2. What hook words or phrases did you see that you'd use to create a segue and guide the discussion?

3. As meeting leader Rene, what will you say to move the meeting forward to a decision?

Potential Answers

1. From this short exchange, it is reasonable to select a consensus-oriented approach to solving the problem because while there is frustration, there is also a willingness to work together to create the proposal.

2. There are six primary hooks in this exchange: client wants; proposal; price-points; documentation about custom color; and documentation about client logo additions, all of which are neutral standing alone. The sixth hook is a question, "Can't anyone help me with this" and is being asked from the engaged enthusiasm ChoiceMark because Marge is asking for a solution to move forward.

3. Rene can move the team forward in a consensus approach that is neutral with a question such as, "Who else can support Marge with information?" Or Rene can support Marge's request from engaged enthusiasm and say, "This is a great client opportunity for the whole company. Let's pull together and support Marge's proposal with all the information she needs."

5. Numbness over Meeting Numbers

Sebastian: Sorry I'm late. The last meeting I was in ran late so I didn't have time to go back to my desk and get the materials for this meeting. And, I got text messages about three problems in the last meeting. By the way, what do we need for this meeting?

Susan: You should have brought your budget for this year and your first quarter results. Lucky for you, you have time now to go get them because Bill had to go round up the projector remote for his presentation and Kim went to get the flipchart from the storage closet. Who knows where Anne is and she called the meeting.

Sebastian: Okay, I'll be right back.

Bill: Found it. Now, if the projector screen will drop down, we'll be able to look at my first quarter report.

Kim: Here's the flipchart. Great, now where are the markers?

Anne: Sorry I'm late. I got hung up in a meeting upstairs. This meeting is for first quarter results reviews and identifying what expenses we can cut back for second quarter.

We need to share information and make decisions in this meeting.

Peter: Make decisions without having a chance to research the impacts of changed budgets? Plus we're 25 minutes into our meeting time and Sebastian isn't back with his stuff...

Sebastian: Sorry. Here I am. I have the first quarter results for the divisions I cover.

Anne: Well...

Questions

1. As Anne the meeting leader, will you use a command-and-control or a consensus-oriented approach?

2. What hook words or phrases did you see that you'd use to create a segue and guide the discussion?

3. As a meeting participant, what will you say to move the meeting forward to a decision?

Potential Answers

1. The meeting has gotten off to an unproductive start. Anne will best serve the team by leading off with a command-and-control set of directions. Once the meeting is back on track and focused on the decisions that can be made in this meeting today, she can shift back into a consensus-oriented approach.

2. Most meeting participants have already demonstrated a consensus-oriented approach to interacting with each other. As a result, any move-the-discussion-forward suggestions will work best when staying in ChoiceMark consensus language such as the following. "We're all here with the right data now, so how about if we focus on the changed dollar amounts first?" or, "Now that we're all ready, what if we spend today's time on the expense lines we think should change? Later we can get with the affected departments to get the information we need to factor into our final recommendations."

6. Concerns Have Surfaced

An emergency problem-solving meeting has been called. Ten team members are in a conference room and don't yet know what the problem is. Mark is the team leader who called the emergency meeting.

Ned: What's going on?

Opal: Yeah, what's so urgent that it can't wait until tomorrow's staff meeting?

Mark: We're getting reports from the floor that equipment is overheating. We need a solution and it can't wait until tomorrow. We can't afford for the line to shut down without having a solution ready to fix it.

Ned: Okay. So what's happening?

Frieder: The molt temperatures are running about five degrees higher than normal.

Opal: What harm do you think will come from this?

Frieder: Serious harm. The temperatures we are running are too high for the equipment we are using. We can't sustain these levels.

Ned: Well, what can we do in a meeting room?

Mark: We can...

Questions

1. As meeting leader Mark, will you use a command-and-control or a consensus-oriented approach?

2. What hook words or phrases did you see that you'd use to create a segue and guide the discussion?

3. What will you say to move the meeting forward to a decision for action?

Potential Answers

1. Mark needs to keep the knowledge of all team members in the room and at the discussion table. Making a command procedural direction, "We can find a solution here in this room," followed by a consensus-oriented direction, "First, let's look at why the temperatures have gone up by five degrees. What's changed in the last 24 hours?" can focus all team members on the decision actions that are needed.

2. There are eight potential hooks that can be built upon to move the discussion in new directions. They are reports from the floor (neutral mindset); equipment is overheating (neutral statement of fact); we need a solution (neutral or engaged enthusiasm); can't afford to shut down without a solution (boxed-in, neutral, or engaged enthusiasm depending on the tone of voice that was used to deliver the message); temperatures are running too high (anti-survival mindset); and too high for the equipment we are using (anti-survival mindset suggesting that we can't fail to address the problem or a disaster will happen); followed by "we can't sustain these levels" (anti-survival); and the question, "What can we do in a meeting room?" (a boxed-in mindset about where and how a solution can be found).

3. "It appears we're in agreement that we have to help find a solution for this temperature and equipment problem right now." Or, anything that restates what the problem is and that a solution needs to be found.

Bringing Both into Daily Use

The preceding chapters and practices have demonstrated that both command-and-control and consensus-driven decision making can be used appropriately depending on the immediate and longer-term needs of a situation. Here are some strategies for you and your organization to bring a balanced use of command-and-control and consensus-driven decision making into daily use. The first strategy is an individual one. As an individual, become a master at meeting and decision-making skills. Without a strong structure and set of processes, every team struggles to focus on its purpose and mission accomplishment. Second, as an individual focus on mastering interpersonal communication skills that will serve you well in a variety of situations, including conflict-filled situations. The third and fourth are team strategies. Third, as a team, set expectations for and reach agreement on the decision discussion tools and approaches you want to be a part of your culture for getting work done. For instance, is your team operating in consensus or command-and-control mode now? Agree on how the team wants to operate going into the future. Finally, as a team establish a ground rule that will guide you when the team is going to shift from consensus-driven to command-and-control decision making or from command and control to consensus. Without this team ground-rule, shifts in approaches may seem arbitrary and can undermine the success of the team.

Commanding Collaborator in Chief

In the February 2007 issue of *Entrepreneur* magazine, an article titled "Building the 21st Century Leader" by Carol Tice described ten skills that are necessary for leadership in this century. Interestingly decisiveness, collaborative skills, and execution of a vision were three of the ten described. The *Moving Out of the Box* decision skills that you are now mastering address all three skill areas. What does the article emphasis tell us? That, as discussed in Chapter 2, being a commanding collaborator in chief is in fact being called for in this century. Recall that a commanding collaborator in chief is a master of both consensus-driven and command-and-control decision making as well as being a master of meeting facilitation and interpersonal communication skills. Here are some job title examples of how being a commanding collaborator in chief can look.

A chief executive officer who has commanding collaborator in chief skills is someone who knows when to make requests, involve others, and consider all inputs as well as when to make a decision and make assignments. And an elected leader who possesses commanding collaborator in chief skills is able to balance input from constituents with subject matter expertise from agencies and multiple sources; create a vision for the future; ask for implementation plans; and cast votes to achieve the vision. The reasons we all need the balanced use of command-and-control decision leadership and consensus-driven decision making are multiple-fold. If more commanding collaborators in chief led organizations, more people would feel valued in their workplaces. If more commanding collaborator in chief decision making occurred in organizations, greater creativity and innovation would likely result. If more commanding collaborator in chief decision making occurred on a daily basis, there would likely be a reduction in national and personal debt.

When Is It Over?

When a project or task is complete, celebrate it and move on. When a decision implementation plan has been successful, celebrate and move on. Too often activities and action items stay on to-do lists even after the activities are no longer needed and the original goals have been achieved. Too many committees and task forces stay alive longer than they are needed. And some teams remain intact even though their missions have been accomplished. Two things happen when individuals and teams fail to determine an answer to the question "when is it over?"

First, emotionally people get drained because of a lack of completion and a sense of never being able to get everything done. Nearly everyone has a longer to-do list than is likely to get done this quarter or this year. So rather than feeling overwhelmed, review the list of your to-do's to determine what needs to come off of the list because you've done it. Also, review the list for things that are done well enough and drop them from your list. Finally, review your to-do list for things that no longer are important to you, your work, or your family and take these items off. You'll discover more energy and experience less stress when your to-do list is shorter and more relevant to your daily life. If you have to-do items and projects that still need to be completed, then by all means keep them on your list and keep going. Take a look at whether you've done all you can do. If you have, determine who needs to see the activity through to completion. Also, determine whether you are the only one who can finish the task. If it is all up to you, plan now for how you'll get it done.

The second thing that happens when a determination of "it's over" hasn't been made is that feeling of "sitting and spinning" where everyone senses that nothing is getting done. Once this attitude sets in, yet again emotional drains begin and now time is lost at the same time as productivity falls. When teams and committees get stuck in "sit-and-spin" mode, it is time to ask "are we done yet?" If the group can't answer this question, try asking, "What needs to happen to show us that we are done?" This question should move the team toward a definition or description that indicates what a finished project looks like. With that picture in mind, the team can work to finish the project and move on.

Celebrating accomplishment is as important as putting an action item onto a to-do list. With the multitasking demands of today's workplace, having a sense of completion is critical to being productive and creative. Review your personal and team project to-do lists. If something is done, celebrate it, check it off your list, and move on. If something is undone, first ask, "Does it still need to be done?" Then, if the task still needs doing, build a plan, and get it done.

Chapter Summary

Team members who are peers now may or may not be peers in the future. This awareness plays into the political behavior that happens in every company, organization, and agency. To achieve greatest effectiveness in the workplace, regardless of your current or future position or job title, master as many tools as possible for leading decision making efforts. Leaving yourself with only the toolbox of skills you currently have limits your future both professionally and personally. The *Moving Out of the Box* tools for decision making conclude with an invitation to keep your resolve for best-possible decision making. In order to achieve best-possible decisions, specifically keep your resolve to make good decisions; master decision tools; stick with decisions made and only revisit them when conditions change or new information becomes available; prompt team members to make decisions rather than allowing others to waffle; and to bring an end to time-wasting meetings that don't lead to clear decisions. Keep moving!

Appendix:
ChoiceMark Questions for
Every Stage of Consensus

Use the questions listed below to enlarge a conversation and move people toward a decision. You'll notice that in some cases, the very same question can be used to get more information and input from each of the five ChoiceMark positions. In all cases, the tone and volume of your voice will make a difference in how well your statements and questions are received. Choose your favorite three to five phrases for each ChoiceMark stage of consensus. Then practice your favorites so that you can speak them confidently into each decision-making conversation you participate in.

Extreme Excitement

As you discovered in Chapter 4, most team leaders think this is where the team needs to be to make a good decision. It's nice, but not required. Use these questions and statements to get team members at the extreme excitement stage to share relevant information and to respect what others have to contribute to the decision and its implementation.

Coming to Consensus—Sharing Information

- What is most compelling about our making this decision?

- What is the best thing that will come out of making this decision?
- You are much more excited about _____ than the rest of us are. What makes you so committed to this action (or decision)?
- Not everyone is likely to get as excited as some of you are about this action, so what examples or experiences can you share that might change our minds?
- Be patient. Let's hear what everyone's perspective is.
- Okay, you've shared your vision. What about everyone else's ideas for making this work?
- We've heard you out. Now, let's hear what others have to say.
- What details are we missing that we should be considering before making a decision?
- Help me understand what leads you to this conclusion.
- How do you know that this is the best course of action?
- Who has done this successfully already?

Reaching a Decision

- Not everyone is in agreement about how to move forward. What can you share with us that might change our minds?
- We have a nonnegotiable deadline. What can you add that will help us make a decision?
- There are more items on the agenda that we need to get to today. Let's focus on making a decision.
- We need to make a go or no-go decision right now. How do you weigh in?
- When do you see implementation occurring?
- What kind of budget will be needed to make this happen?
- What project plan will we need to make this work?
- When are the deadlines going to be?
- Where will the resources come from for implementation?

Decision Implementation

- Who can help get this done?
- Share your vision for the rollout please.
- Please start the project timeline for us.
- Now that the team has agreed on the decision, what are you going to do to implement it?
- What are you committed to doing to implement this decision?
- Now that you've made your decision, how can the rest of us support implementation?
- What help do you want or need in order to get things done?

- Now that we've completed the project, what went well? What could we have improved?

When You Are in Extreme Excitement, Ask Others:

- What are your thoughts?
- What are your ideas?
- What ideas should I also be taking into consideration?
- What experiences have you had with problems like this?
- What results have you seen in the past?
- How can I avoid any barriers that have happened in the past?
- What other approaches might work?
- Where could we visit to see the ideas in action?
- When is a realistic timetable for implementation?
- How many resources will we need?
- Where in our own organization is this already working?

Engaged Enthusiasm

When you can get the team into this state of being, chances are that a decision followed by implementation will result. Use these questions to ensure that relevant information has been shared with the team and to ensure that enthusiasm doesn't wane after the meeting ends. Chapter 5 is where the engaged enthusiasm details are found.

Coming to Consensus—Sharing Information

- What is it that has you so committed to making the decision this way?
- What else can you share with us that might make us as inspired as you are to move forward this way?

- What has convinced you that this is the best course of action?
- What information can you share with us that might persuade us to your point of view?
- Where have you seen this work successfully?
- Help me understand what leads you to this conclusion.
- What details are we missing that we should be considering before making a decision?

Reaching a Decision

- Once you've reached neutral, will you stay here?
- Not everyone is in agreement about how to move forward. What can you share with us that might change our minds?
- We have a nonnegotiable deadline. What can you add that will help us make a decision?
- There are more items on the agenda that we need to get to today. Let's focus on making a decision.
- We need to make a go or no-go decision right now. How do you weigh in?
- Which subject matter experts will need to review our plans?

Decision Implementation

- Please tell us about your vision for implementing this decision.
- Now that the team has agreed on the decision, what are you going to do to implement it?
- Now that you've made your decision, how can the rest of us support implementation?
- What help do you want or need in order to get things done?
- Where will we find the resources and staffing to accomplish this?
- When is it realistic to move ahead with this plan?
- What timeline do you envision as being realistic?
- Who else will be available to help with implementation?
- Now that we've completed the project, what went well? What could we have improved?

When You Are in Engaged Enthusiasm, Ask Others:

- What experiences have you had with this situation?
- What can you tell us about making sure implementation is successful?
- When has our company tried this in the past? How did things go?
- Please share your ideas on how this can be improved.
- Please offer your suggestions for implementation.

- How much information can you share without violating any confidentiality agreements?
- Which resources will we need to implement the decision successfully?
- Who else can help us build our implementation plan?
- Where can we look for lessons from similar situations?
- What barriers do you see that might prevent this from happening successfully?
- What problems have arisen in the past when an idea like this was implemented?
- Who can I talk to about any downsides of the proposal?

Neutral

When someone, or the whole team, is neither excited nor negative, you are seeing neutral. Don't worry because sometimes this isn't a bad place to be to make a good decision. Use these questions to uncover concerns, to discover whether anyone will stand in the way if the rest of the team moves forward, or to recover a team member who wants to move to anti-survival. Chapter 6 details the neutral stage of consensus.

Coming to Consensus—Sharing Information

- What concerns do you have about making this decision?
- What questions do you have?
- What expertise or insight do you have on this?
- Who else should we be consulting with to get accurate information?
- Tell us what other information you'd like.
- What details are we missing that we should be considering before making a decision?
- Where would you suggest we go to gather more information that might change our approach?
- Do you know of anyone or any teams that we can go to for insight? Who?

Reaching a Decision

- Not everyone is in agreement about how to move forward. What can you share with us that might change our minds?
- We have a nonnegotiable deadline. What can you add that will help us make a decision?
- There are more items on the agenda that we need to get to today. Let's focus on making a decision.
- We need to make a go or no-go decision right now. How do you weigh in?
- When will your project load have an opening that would allow your participation on this project?

Decision Implementation

- Now that the team has agreed on the decision, what are you going to do to implement it?
- Now that you've made your decision, how can the rest of us support implementation?
- Will you stand in the way or prevent implementation from happening?
- What help do you want or need in order to take action?
- Now that we've completed the project, what went well? What could we have improved?
- Is this project one you'd be willing to participate in?
- What element of this decision might you help us implement?

When You Are in Neutral, Ask Others:

- What leads you to believe this won't work?
- What leads you to believe this will work?
- Why should anyone feeling boxed-in or in anti-survival shift their positions?
- Why should team members in engaged enthusiasm or in extreme excitement shift their positions?
- How can we find a middle ground?
- What decision could work for everyone?
- What information do we still need in order to make this decision?
- What can you share that could persuade me to your point of view?
- Where can we go to get the information we need to make a decision one way or the other?
- When does the decision absolutely have to be made?
- What deadlines can we negotiate?

Boxed-in

This is the stage when an individual or an entire team is stuck and can't come up with fresh ideas. The concerns expressed here may change the decision outcome, so it is important to listen and learn. Use these questions to uncover concerns and barriers. And use them to support the team's best-possible decision making. Chapter 7 focuses on boxed-in thinking.

Coming to Consensus—Sharing Information

- What should we be considering that we're overlooking right now?
- What experiences have you had that tell you that this might not work?
- What details are we missing that we should be considering before making a decision?
- What can you tell us about what went wrong last time?
- What needs to change to make it work this time?
- What modifications might make this work?
- Where did things break down last time?
- What lessons were learned last time that we can use to not make the same mistakes?
- Who else experienced these challenges? Shall we get them to share their expertise too?
- What expertise will prevent us from going down the same path that failed last time?
- Where can we find the details?

Reaching a Decision

- Not everyone is in agreement about how to move forward. What can you share with us that might change our minds?
- We have a nonnegotiable deadline. What can you add that will help us make a decision?
- There are more items on the agenda that we need to get to today. Let's focus on making a decision.
- We need to make a go or no-go decision right now. How do you weigh in?

Decision Implementation

- Now that you've made your decision, how can you support the rest of us implementing our decision?
- Will you stand in the way or prevent implementation from happening?
- What help can you offer to get things done?
- Now that we've completed the project, what went well? What could we have improved?

When You Are in Boxed-in, Ask Others:

- What experiences have you had that suggest this will work?
- What are you seeing that I'm not?
- When could this work?
- How can the approach you all are discussing really work?
- Where has this approach worked?
- What timetables for implementation do you envision? Are they realistic?
- Who has been successful with this approach? Is there an example company we can study?
- Are you willing to hear out my concerns?
- May I please share my experiences as to why this won't work as planned?

Anti-Survival

This is the stage when an individual, a group, or an entire team is saying, "No, we shouldn't do this." Sometimes they are right. Use these questions to learn how to listen to the message at hand and how to ensure that anti-survival thinking has been heard and taken into consideration when making the final decision and asking for follow-up action and implementation to occur. Chapter 8 is the focus on anti-survival mindsets.

Coming to Consensus—Sharing Information

- What experiences have you had that tell you that this will not work?
- What details are we missing that we should be considering before making a decision?
- What harm do you see coming from this approach?
- Where can we look for examples of things failing in the way you are predicting?
- What research can be done to overcome the challenges and concerns?
- How can the concerns be overcome?
- When is a system like we are talking about most likely to fail?
- Who is likely to get hurt if we proceed?
- What systems are likely to break down if we proceed?
- What harm will come to the environment if we proceed?

Reaching a Decision

- Not everyone is in agreement about how to move forward. What can you share with us that might change our minds?
- We have a nonnegotiable deadline. What can you add that will help us make a decision?
- There are more items on the agenda that we need to get to today. Let's focus on making a decision.
- We need to make a go or no-go decision right now. How do you weigh in?
- What methods of prevention can we use to ensure problems do not come up?

Decision Implementation

- Will you stand in the way or prevent implementation from happening?
- What help can you offer to get things done?
- How can we make modifications to prevent harm from occurring?
- Now that we've completed the project, what went well? What could we have improved?

When You Are in Anti-Survival, Ask Others:

- Have you seen this work? Where?
- What is driving this exact decision?
- When does the decision absolutely have to be made? Maybe we can talk through more options.
- Where can we see that this plan has been safely implemented?
- What safety record can you show me to ease my concerns?

- What are two alternate approaches to solving this problem that are less likely to cause harm?
- Have the regulations changed?
- Have our company policies changed such that we can pursue this option?
- Because I still have reservations, I'm hoping you can provide examples of where this has really worked.
- Are you open to modifying the approach?
- How can we modify the approach so that it can work without causing harm?

Index

About the Author

JANA M. KEMP is the founder of Meeting & Management Essentials, which focuses on improving productivity, morale, and profit through improving meeting, time, and decision-management skills for individuals and organizations. Kemp draws on over 20 years of working in the human resources development and facilitation fields for her work with clients. She is also a meeting facilitator, public speaker, and veteran author. Kemp's second book, *No! How One Simple Word Can Transform Your Life,* has been translated into Polish, Dutch, Turkish, Arabic, and Chinese. She is also the author of *Building Community in Buildings* (Praeger) and the forthcoming *Prepared Not Paranoid* (Praeger). Kemp has also had a career in broadcasting. For four years, she originated and hosted business-radio talk show *Momentum,* interviewing business people from across the country, and she has provided business segments on NBC's Boise Affiliate KTVB Channel 7's *Sunrise Program* and KSVT's *This Week in Sun Valley.* A graduate of the Idaho Police Academy, Kemp entered elected public service for the first time in 2004 when she was elected to one term in the Idaho House of Representatives. Learn more at www.janakemp.com.